THE MAGNA MAN

THE MAGNA MAN

MY ROAD TO ECONOMIC FREEDOM

◇◇◇◇◇◇◇

FRANK STRONACH

WITH PAUL PIVATO

HARPERCOLLINS PUBLISHERS LTD

*To a remarkable woman
and the mother of my children, Elfriede Stronach.*

*To my children and my grandchildren: my daughter, Belinda,
and son, Andy; my grandson, Frank; and my granddaughters,
Nikki and Selena. I am very proud of all of you. I am confident
that you will grow the family business entrusted to you, and that
you will give some of your time and money, as I have always tried
to do, in order to help build a better society.*

CONTENTS

THE MAGNA MAN

L ife is truly a question of fate and circumstances. If you are at the right place, at the right time, with the right sort of ingredients, a lot of great things can happen.

Consider my own life. I was born during the Great Depression and grew up in a small town at the foot of the Alps in southeastern Austria. Both my parents were factory workers. My mother sold vegetables that she grew on a small piece of land near our home to bring in a few extra dollars. My father was a labour activist. From my mother, I learned the value of hard work and the entrepreneurial spirit. From my father, I learned a sense of fairness and concern for people that would shape my thinking later in life. When I was 14, just over one year after the Second World War had ended, my no-nonsense mother took me by the hand to the factory where she worked, and I began my apprenticeship as a tool and die maker—an event that altered the course my life.

When I turned 21, I had a strong thirst to see the world, and I left my homeland and immigrated to Canada. My first job was washing dishes and peeling potatoes in the basement of a hospital kitchen—and I remember feeling so sorry for myself. After several years of journeyman work as a toolmaker, I scraped together enough money to strike out on my own. I opened a small tool shop in a rented garage, and during the first few years I worked sixteen hours a day, seven days a week, sleeping at night on a fold-up cot next to my lathe. As a young immigrant struggling to build a new life in the New World, I never for a moment imagined that I would one day accomplish all that I have done since then.

I built a company from scratch that is today recognized as the premier automotive supplier in the world. Magna International Inc. is the world's most diversified supplier of automobile components, generating close to $30 billion in annual sales, with no debt and $1 billion cash sitting in the bank. The company produces parts for virtually every car and truck on the road today, and even designs and builds complete vehicles for companies such as Mercedes-Benz, BMW and Peugeot. Magna builds so many cars, in fact, that it is now the world's largest independent assembler of vehicles.

The factories and R & D centres that are part of the automotive giant I founded now number more than 380 in twenty-six countries around the world, employing 115,000 people—assembly line workers, designers, engineers of every stripe and one of the largest concentrations of toolmakers inside any company on earth. In towns like Victor, Iowa, and Saltillo, Mexico, and Ebergassing, Austria, Magna employees produce everything from pulleys and plastic panels to seats and sensors. They stamp metal parts such as shock towers and engine cradles for the steel underbelly of the car, pump out plastic bumpers by the millions, assemble dashboards and complete cockpits, and make mirrors with electronic chips that can tell drivers everything from the temperature outside to the vehicle's tire pressure. These highly engineered parts and modules are stamped and punched and moulded by presses so large they could never fit under the roof of that first garage where Magna was born.

Life has been incredibly good to me. I've met kings and queens, presidents and prime ministers, the rich and the famous, a lot of colourful characters, and plenty of decent, down-to-earth people. Even though I've experienced the lowest of the lows and the highest of the highs, it is the hardships I've endured that have made me the person I am today, and taught me the business lessons that helped me grow Magna into an auto parts empire. I've lived under the boot of two of the most brutal regimes the world has ever seen—all within the span of just a few years. I've known hunger and hardship. I've been fired and laid off and discriminated against. All of those experiences have left deep impressions.

The secret to success in business is disarmingly simple, and it is contained in the motto that Magna lives by: *Make a better product for a better price.* In a world awash in mediocrity, it is an unbeatable prescription for making profits and rising to the top. But it is hard to achieve on a consistent basis, and making a better product at a better price requires a commitment to excellence, efficiency and innovation that can only come about when people have a stake in the outcome—when they own a piece of the machinery they're working on, and get a slice of the profits they produce.

Over the years, I've accumulated a lot of wealth, and in the process I've opened the door for thousands and thousands of people to earn a good income. The profit and ownership formula known as "Fair Enterprise" that I created has fuelled

Magna's growth and made millionaires out of many people, most of whom were immigrants like me. It has generated hefty returns for investors and given Magna the wherewithal to donate hundreds of millions of dollars to charities, social causes and community projects in the many small towns where our employees live and work.

But what I am most proud of—the source of my greatest satisfaction—is the fact that I have helped to create more than 100,000 jobs. The companies I've built have provided meaningful employment to individuals and families all over the world. It is an indescribable feeling—beyond compare.

I am the son of working-class parents, a tradesman who came to these shores with rudimentary English and barely any business know-how. If I could accomplish all that I have done in my life with a very limited education and modest means, I believe many others could do the same. The human mind has an incredible capacity for ingenuity and creativity, and I'm a firm believer that we all possess enormous untapped potential. If you walk in my footsteps and follow the simple formula for success I've spelled out in this book, then I'm confident your business could be among the very best in its industry and that you could be a more effective business leader.

In the pages ahead, I share with you the many hard-won lessons I've learned and the many extraordinary experiences I've accumulated. I wrote this book in the hope that you will draw some inspiration and insight from the path I've taken as you pursue your own road to happiness and fulfillment.

CHAPTER 1

THE RIGHT PLACE, THE RIGHT TIME
AND THE RIGHT INGREDIENTS

Life is a question of fate and circumstances. If you are in the right place at the right time with the right ingredients, a lot of great things can happen.

I immigrated to Canada in 1954 with nothing more than a suitcase, a few hundred dollars and a dream to build a better life.

I sailed on a one-way ticket from Rotterdam in late April of that year on an old Dutch freighter named *Groote Beer*, together with hundreds of other young Europeans, all of us hungry to build a new life for ourselves in North America. We bunked four to a cabin. I was 21 years old, and I can still recall, as if it were yesterday, my anxiety and sense of anticipation as the ship pulled away from the dock, its horn blasting. At one point, I even thought of diving off the deck and swimming back to shore before the ship sailed too far from the harbour and out toward the vast expanse of ocean. But I had read and heard too many stories about young men and women who went to the New World and hit it big. I wanted to be one of those people.

It was early in the morning when the ship arrived in Quebec City about nine days later. As we sailed up the St. Lawrence River I could see the low-rising hills along the shores still dotted with patches of snow, and I remember thinking how massive and imposing the terrain looked. I thought, *This is how Christopher Columbus must have felt.* When we finally docked, I was so relieved to feel the solid ground beneath my feet. We filed into long lines, and a Canadian immigration officer stamped my passport and handed me a railroad ticket to Montreal. I arrived at the downtown train station a few hours later. I had never seen anything so large in all my life. I didn't know which way to turn, or where to exit. Clutching my small suitcase, I began walking the streets of what was then Canada's biggest city, feeling alone and full of wonder about what my future might hold.

I had just one thought on my mind: finding room and board. I only had a few hundred bucks, and I would have burned through my cash pretty quickly if I'd stayed in a hotel. I knew enough English to get by and I looked for signs that read "Room for Let." I knocked on door after door and asked if they had a room. But I had no luck. Perhaps it was because I was seasick for most of the voyage to Canada, and I looked ragged and run down, or perhaps some people didn't want to rent to an immigrant fresh off the boat. But after about an hour or two of walking the streets and banging on doors, I finally found a room.

Early the next morning, I started searching for work. I looked for factories, because factory work was what I knew. I was willing to do anything. I knocked on the doors of around thirty companies. After several days of coming up empty-handed, I began to worry and went to an unemployment office. One of the workers there told me that a golf course was looking for someone to retrieve golf balls at the driving range and he gave me the address. I got on a bus and rode for the better part of a day, searching in vain for the golf course. Little did I know that golf courses are not on public bus routes! I was young and athletic, and I sometimes wonder, had I found that course, whether I might have ended up becoming a pro golfer.

I was worried and frustrated. After two weeks, my money was dwindling. I talked to other immigrants and none of them had found jobs either. The country was in the midst of a recession, and the people seemed a little edgier, a little tenser than back home. I didn't know anybody. And there was no work. I hadn't eaten in a day or so, and I had lost a lot of weight since I arrived. As far as I was concerned, it was the end of the line. So I took what little cash I had and bought a Greyhound bus ticket to Kitchener, a small city located halfway between Detroit and Toronto. I had the address of a fellow I knew from Weiz, a toolmaker named Max Windhager who used to work at the factory where I had apprenticed.

Kitchener had a strong German heritage and a large pocket of German-speaking immigrants. It was at one time known as Berlin, but in World War I, when Canadian soldiers were fighting in the trenches against the Germans, the government of the day renamed the city after a popular British general. I got off the bus in the main square and spent the better part of the day wandering around town, tired and hungry. It's a lot different being hungry because you want to lose some weight than being hungry because you can't afford to buy food. Those kind of experiences leave lasting scars. I kept pulling the slip of paper with Max's name and address out of my pocket, and thinking, *I hope the guy still lives here, because if he doesn't, I don't know what the hell I'm going to do.*

I was beginning to get desperate. I remember thinking: *So this is the capitalist system?* Maybe my left-leaning father was right. Here I was, a skilled tradesman itching to work, but I couldn't find anything. It's not my nature to ask anyone for help. But I had reached the point where I was ready to beg. I knocked on Max's door. He opened the door, smiled and said, "Hello, Frank. Good to see you again. How are you? C'mon in. You look hungry." They were welcome words.

A few days later, I got my first job: washing dishes and peeling potatoes and carrots in the basement of a hospital. I scoured and scrubbed from 6 a.m. to 6 p.m., with one day off per week. I made $80 per month and got room and board at the hospital. Here I was, a young buck, rinsing plates all day with a bunch of sweet old ladies.

On Saturdays, I would head out for a night on the town at Club Berlin. There was a lot of slow dancing in those days, and sometimes the girls I was dancing with would ask me what I did for a living. "I work in a hospital," I would say. And the girls would usually say, "Your hands are so smooth. Are you a surgeon?" Sometimes I would play along, but I would always eventually tell them the truth, that I was really just a dishwasher. When I said that, most of them didn't want to dance as close anymore—after all, what girl wants to go out with a dishwasher? But those that stayed close—that was true love!

After a few weeks, Max helped get me a job as a machinist at a plant that made components for the ill-fated Avro Arrow fighter jet. I worked there about seven or eight months and then got laid off. So I drove to Oakville, just west of Toronto, where Ford Motor Company had recently built a massive new vehicle assembly plant and was hiring toolmakers. I filled out some applications and was interviewed by someone who told me that I looked awfully young, that I couldn't have too much experience and that my chances of being hired by Ford were next to nil. Nowadays, I occasionally meet with the CEO of Ford Canada, and I sometimes joke that if I had been hired back then, I might now have his job.

After failing to latch on with Ford, I hitchhiked to Toronto. I asked the guy who gave me a ride to take me to one of the cheaper hotels in the city. He dropped me off at the corner of Jarvis and Dundas streets, right across from the Warwick Hotel. I had a beer and a hamburger in the basement tavern. It was a pretty rowdy joint: blue-collar workers, hookers and some rough characters. People were getting drunk on cheap draft, hollering and laughing. After weeks of washing dishes in the hospital basement, Toronto was a refreshing change, a wild and raucous town. I got a room for ten bucks but didn't sleep too well, what with all the coming and going, the shouting and slamming of doors. A few weeks later, some of my friends from Kitchener came to Toronto to visit me, craving a taste of big-city life. They said, "Hey, Frank, where's that rowdy hotel you told us about?" So we got in the car and drove around for hours looking for the Warwick, but try as we might, we couldn't find the notorious landmark.

I followed up on a few ads in the paper and found work at auto parts manufacturer A.G. Simpson—at the time, one of the biggest in the country. It was my first job in Canada as a toolmaker, and I bought a toolbox along with some basic drills, files and gauges. I was hired together with a handful of other toolmakers for some rush orders the company needed to fill. After about three or four months of working at A.G. Simpson, I got laid off. One afternoon the foreman came up to me and said don't bother coming back the next day—just like that.

What happened next was a turning point for me. I found work with a small tool shop in downtown Toronto, located in a rundown block with a lot of old brick factories, not far from the Riverdale Zoo. I started in the spring of 1955 and worked there until the end of 1956. Altogether, there were around ten of us, mostly Austrians, including the owner. It was not long before the owner made me manager of the operation, and it was then that I got my first real taste of what it would be like to run my own business. Not long after, the owner offered me a partnership. His proposal was a bit vague and wishy-washy, but still very appealing. We never got around to hammering out an agreement. It wasn't his fault—work got busy, time rushed by. But by then something had changed: I started gaining confidence. I starting thinking that it's not such a big deal to set up your own shop. There's nothing to it, being in business for yourself—*I can do this.* My appetite was whetted, and my dream of starting my own business was, for the first time, within grasp. From that moment onward, there was no looking back.

◇◇◇◇◇

It was 1957. Elvis Presley, one of my favourite singers, was number one on the music charts. The baby boom was in full swing. And an average new car sold for around two grand.

Three years after arriving in Canada at the age of 21, I had finally scraped together enough money to open my own small tool and die shop. It was located inside an old one-storey building known as the Gatehouse, in the heart of Toronto's manufacturing district. The shop had battered wooden floorboards and was the size of a four-car garage. I bought a used drill press, a small lathe and milling machine, a band saw and surface grinder. The total price for the equipment was around $12,000. I put down $3,000 of my own money and made payments on the balance. I opened a bank account and a line of credit at the Bank of Nova Scotia on St. Clair Avenue, not far from the factory. The bank manager was a fellow named George Hitchman, who would years later serve on the board of directors of Magna International. George was an old-school banker, somewhat stern but fair. "How much do you intend to deposit?" he asked gruffly. I gave him $3,000 cash and he approved a $1,000 overdraft. Once all the paperwork was signed, he shook my hand and said, "I'm going to keep a close eye on you, young man."

Within that old garage I had everything I needed. To save money, I would buy off-cuts, lower-priced leftover pieces of metal. I kept a small drafting table and desk over in one corner for sketching tool designs and scrawling out invoices. I had a toilet and a sink, a little fridge and a hot plate. In the mornings, I filled a can with warm water and soap and used a sponge to wash myself.

I worked sixteen hours a day, seven days a week, and slept on a small foldaway cot that I kept next to my lathe. I remember getting out of bed some nights to go to the washroom, tiptoeing in my bare feet over the jagged metal shards that lay on the floor near the milling machine. I usually worked until about 10 or 11 p.m., and once in a while, after shutting down the machines, I would meet some friends at a tavern or café just to clear my head and have a few laughs. For dinner, I often cooked some canned food on the hot plate. Just a few hundred yards down the road from my shop was an Italian deli. It had huge wheels of cheese on the floor that small kids from the neighbourhood would stand on while their moms picked up cuts of meat at the counter. Once I bought a chunk of sausage and some fresh-baked bread and brought it back to the shop. I left the sausage on my bench for a minute and went to wash my hands. When I came back, I saw a rat scurrying away with the meat. I threw a piece of steel at the rat as it scampered down a hole in the wooden floorboards.

I called my shop Accurate Tool and Die, but not long after I started I got a letter in the mail from a lawyer representing a company called Accurate Mould. They said I would have to change the name or they would sue me. So I changed it to Multimatic.

In those early years, I had only one desire—to become economically free, so that I would never be hungry again and never have to crawl from anybody.

I was determined to make my new business a success. I hustled and went knocking on doors looking for orders. One of my first jobs was for American Standard, the large U.S. firm that makes bathroom and kitchen products such as tubs, toilets and faucets. They needed a complicated bracket to hang a sink tub and said to me, "See what you can come up with. If you solve that, we might have some more work for you." I went back to my shop, sketched out some prototypes, and three weeks later came back with a machined tool that punched out brackets. I made $3,000—about four times what I would have made working at a tool shop for someone else. My newest customer was happy with the work and ended up giving me more business.

I would go into nearby factories and speak to the foreman to try to drum up some orders. I won new business by promising my customers that I could solve their problems and I backed up my promise with an ironclad guarantee: if the customers were not satisfied, they would not have to pay me. That can-do attitude has never changed—more than fifty years later, we ask Magna's customers in Detroit and Frankfurt and Tokyo, "What are your problems? How can we help you?" And then we go straight to work to find a solution.

Those early days were tough. I did everything from sales and bookkeeping to machinery maintenance and product delivery. One time I was sweeping the floor in my oil-stained overalls when a man walked in and asked if I would take him to meet the boss. "You're speaking to him," I said.

I got a lot of contracts, and sometimes I underestimated how long it would take to do the job. I once worked seventy-two hours straight through without stopping. But it wasn't for the money. It was because I had made a commitment and wanted to keep my word. I once got an order from an auto parts supplier north of the city to make a tool used to manufacture tire jacks. It was a rush job, and I worked forty-eight hours around the clock to fill the order. It was a snowy winter day, and on the way up to my customer's office I fell asleep at the wheel and drove my Chevy into a ditch. Luckily, I wasn't hurt. With my heart racing and now wide awake, I managed to deliver the tools on time, as promised. It was a trait that over the years became deeply rooted in the Magna culture: we did whatever it took to deliver the goods on time.

I hired my first employee after one month. He ended up becoming a general manager at one of our factories, Hy-Prod, ten years later, and he stayed with Magna for over thirty years, right up until the day he retired. That first year, I made around $20,000—a very good wage. I kept bringing in new orders and hiring more and more people. After about eight months, with some savings tucked away in the bank, I moved out of the garage into a bachelor apartment to make room for more equipment and machines. By the end of the year, I had ten workers on my payroll. Every single one of them ended up becoming Magna plant managers.

Joining me at the shop on most weekends was an old friend from my hometown of Weiz, Anton Czapka. Tony had arrived by boat like me, landing in Montreal. He showed up at my door in Kitchener one day, the same way I did at Max Windhager's place, and slept on my couch until he was able to get work.

Tony was very down-to-earth and never put on airs. He also had a big heart. When I first told him about my plans to open my own shop, he enthusiastically encouraged me: "Do it, Frank." He gave me a wad of bills, $5,000 in total, and said, "Take it. Put it in the bank." He completely trusted me and had confidence that I could make a go of it. His chunk of cash was working capital and gave me the resources I needed to strike out on my own sooner than I would have been able to otherwise. I could never have done it without him. Tony not only became a partner, he became my closest and most trusted friend.

One of my first customers was an auto parts plant in Ajax, close to the shore of Lake Ontario, just east of Toronto. The manager was a tall, lanky and easy-going American named Burt Pabst who had a real flair for marketing. Burt was from Detroit and sent a lot of his tooling to my shop in Toronto. After a while, Burt eventually joined my growing business, driving into Toronto on weeknights to help out. We were making so many tools for the production of auto parts that we started thinking, *Why not make the parts as well?* That way, we'd make profits on both the tooling and the parts.

By the end of the first full year of business, the hard work began to pay off: the new company had approximately $150,000 in sales. We plowed most of the money we made during the first year back into the business to buy materials and pay off the loan that we had taken out to buy used machinery. I loved those days, often working late into the night with the guys. I'd go buy a bucket of fried chicken and a case of beer, and we'd all pitch in to get the job done.

We worked hard and we worked long hours, but we always had a few laughs. I remember, for instance, the very first day on the job for a certain new hire, a young guy from Germany. When we broke for lunch, he went to the store and bought a can of what he thought was meatloaf. He started gulping down forkfuls of the meat, and said, "Geez, the meat looks so delicious in the photo on the can, but it tastes like crap." The guys around the lunch table burst out laughing, and then one of them began barking, "Woof, woof." After a while, even the new guy joined in the laughter.

It was during the second full year of operations that an event occurred that forever changed our course. In 1959, we landed our first auto parts contract: an order from General Motors to produce metal-stamped sun visor brackets. I would take turns with the other employees, working long into the night on a single punch press to meet a shipment deadline the next day. I then delivered the parts to the General Motors assembly plant in Oshawa early the next morning in my used 1955 Chevy. We packed so many boxes of metal brackets into the car that the tires looked as if they were flat.

In total, we produced several hundred thousand brackets at a price of around 40 cents per part, pocketing a few pennies on each piece we made. The total contract was worth about $80,000. We built the tool, put the tool on a punch press, fed the sheet metal in and ran it through the punch press, and out came the sun visor brackets. We made deliveries three times a week, shipping batches of about 5,000 brackets at a time. The presses were thumping day and night, and we were practically climbing over each other in that bustling shop.

More contracts from General Motors soon followed, as well as contracts from Ford and Chrysler. These were the glory years of the North American car industry. Detroit's "Big Three" were booming, and we started feeding them the parts they needed to meet North America's insatiable desire for cars. In our little shop with the wooden floorboards, the metal parts clanging into steel bins sounded like coins cascading into a bucket.

PUT IT IN WRITING

When I was manager of a tool shop, the owner one day offered me a partnership. The terms of the partnership were a bit vague but still very appealing. However, the owner never got around to presenting me with a written offer. Not long after, I left and started my own business. Several years later, the manager of one of my factories told me he wanted to leave and start his own business. I didn't want to lose him, so I offered him a share of the ownership and a cut of the profits, and he agreed. I had learned a valuable lesson from the time when I was offered a partnership: if you're serious about your offer, put it in writing.

CHAPTER 2

THE MAGNA SUCCESS FORMULA: SHARING PROFITS AND OWNERSHIP

Magna is much more than a company. It is a whole new economic culture.

A year after the first auto parts contract, we had doubled in size to twenty people. And a year after that, my small business was growing so quickly that we moved from our small rented garage to a new factory in the suburbs north of Toronto. It was a 3,000-square-foot plant, and I drafted the plans, contracted the work and supervised the construction.

One day I noticed that my foreman, Herman Koob, was acting a little oddly, so I asked him what was wrong. "Well," he said, "I've been thinking about starting my own business." Herman felt much the same way that I did when I was managing someone else's tool and die shop several years earlier. He was itching to go out on his own, to be his own boss. But I didn't want to lose a top-notch operator like Herman.

I could have doubled his salary, but it would have been only a temporary fix. It would not have filled the hunger he had to be

17

an owner—to run his own show. There's something special about ownership that goes much deeper than mere financial gain.

I realized that if Herman left, his departure would stifle the company's growth. I also realized that if I hired a new foreman, and I didn't show him all the ropes on how to run the business, then I would end up still doing most of the work, and I didn't like that prospect very much. My next thought was that if I taught the new foreman everything I knew, he might eventually want to leave and start his own business too, the same way I did, and the same way Herman felt. So I came up with a simple solution: I asked Herman to become a partner in the business. I had learned two valuable lessons from the time, a few years earlier, when I was offered a partnership that never materialized. The first lesson was to put any serious offer in writing. The second lesson was to make the terms of the partnership agreement crystal clear. The next day I sat down with Herman and said, "Why don't we open up a new factory and you could have a one-third ownership?" We drafted an agreement fairly quickly. He would get a base salary and no more overtime. I said, "Look, you've got to hustle, and if you make a profit, you get a portion and I get a portion."

Herman did not have a lot of money to invest, but he had a lot of drive and initiative. I opened a second factory, Dieomatic, with Herman in charge. We put up the money needed to build the factory, bought the machinery and made Herman a part owner.

The new factory was a great success. In two years, the number of employees at Dieomatic grew from ten to fifty. Because he was a part owner, Herman hustled day and night. He made the business grow. And the more business he drummed up, the more money he made. So I took the next foreman and did the same thing, and then I took another foreman and gave him the same deal, and after a while I had a growing number of factories, and all the managers at those factories had a cut of the business. Like Herman Koob, they were all first-rate operators, nuts-and-bolts guys who could run the factory and turn a profit making just about any part under the sun. All of a sudden, there I was, a young guy with a bunch of factories under my belt and more money than I ever imagined.

The partnership arrangement became the blueprint for Magna's unique decentralized operating structure, where each Magna plant was an independent business unit that was run by a hands-on manager who received a portion of the factory's profits. We had hit upon a winning formula—one that Harvard Business School would years later describe in a case study as "Magna's success formula."

I had an even simpler way to describe it: I called it giving everyone a piece of the action.

◇◇◇◇◇

Seven years after first arriving in Canada, I was heartsick for home and needed a break. In the years since I had left, I had sent my parents and friends the odd postcard or letter, but for the most part I was too wrapped up trying to build my small business.

It was the spring of 1961, and the small tool and die shop I started four years earlier now had several new factories and about $500,000 in annual sales. The days of sleeping in the factory and cooking meals on a hot plate were over. So after working day in and day out for many years, I was finally able to take some time off and return home.

I traded in my used 1955 Chevy and bought my first new car: a glossy black Pontiac Parisienne, two tons of chrome and metal, with a sleek body and tail lights that made the car look like a rocket ship. I drove the car to New York, where I boarded the S.S. *United States* and set sail for northern France, with my car tucked away in the belly of the ship. Once I got to France, I spent the next day and a half driving through the farmlands, fields and mountains to my hometown of Weiz, Austria.

It was close to midnight when I approached the town where I was born and raised. I was driving on a gravel road in the foothills, and as I came around a curve I suddenly saw the scattered lights of the town in the valley below. I pulled over, got out and leaned against the car, the hood still hot beneath the palms of my hands. I stood there for about half an hour, looking down into the valley. I did not look back in anger or resentment at the poverty and harshness of my upbringing. I counted my many blessings, and I was deeply grateful for all of the twists and turns that my life had taken, not knowing where it would carry me or what path lay ahead. I felt that I was the luckiest man in the world. In the cool stillness of the night, my mind was flooded with a thousand memories and emotions.

I thought of my mother, who rented a small plot of land and grew cucumbers, tomatoes, radishes and onions and then sold them at the market. Wartime food rationing meant hunger and deprivation for many families. On most days, she made us porridge-like cornmeal for breakfast and cornmeal for lunch, sometimes with soup or a salad. Once in a while, as a special treat, she would drizzle hot bacon grease and bits of bacon over top the cornmeal—a dish I still make myself today, alone in my kitchen on a rainy Sunday afternoon.

As a young boy, the only thing on my mind was playing

soccer. But as I got older my mother always harped at me, saying that I needed to learn a trade. She would give me chores—sweeping floors, weeding the gardens, cutting wood. If I didn't follow through, she would occasionally whack me with a carpet beater. As I grew older and stronger, I was able to hold her arms and stave off the beating, and I could see her trying her hardest not to laugh.

She always bought shoes a few sizes larger so they would last longer, and she got upset at me when I kicked stones along the road as we walked into town. She would say, "Boy, you have to stop kicking those stones. You're wearing the shoes out."

I also thought of my father. A muscular man with blondish-brown hair, he apprenticed as a miller in a flour mill and also worked as a lathe operator and at countless other factory jobs. He was a bit of a dreamer, a bookworm and an idealist who believed in the brotherhood of man and who railed against the elites of the day. I could see him sitting beside the radio, turning the dial, trying to find foreign broadcasts, which were forbidden during the war.

But what I thought about most, looking down into the valley below, was that after all the struggles of starting my own business and settling into a new country thousands of miles away, after all the long nights and weekends and sacrifices, I had finally made it. I didn't have to worry ever again about being hungry or being fired or having a roof over my head—all of those fears and anxieties my parents grappled with when I was growing up and that I later experienced myself. I was a free man!

It was around midnight when I arrived at my mother's home. I hadn't told her I was coming; I wanted to surprise her. I knocked on the window shutter and heard her ask, "Who is it?" I simply said, "It's me." My mother immediately recognized her son's voice, and she let out a long-drawn-out cry of joy and surprise.

The next day, I hooked up with some old friends and we piled into my Parisienne and drove around town, drawing the wide-eyed stares of locals, who turned their heads to catch a glimpse of the car as it wound its way through the narrow cobblestone streets. I wasn't trying to show off, like some big shot who had struck it rich. I knew my childhood buddies would get a big kick out of driving in the car. For me, just watching the looks on their faces, their shouts to the townsfolk as we passed by, that was sheer joy. We all felt like we had just won the big game and were carrying home the championship cup. We stopped at local taverns and cafés, the way we used to in years gone by, and we hoisted celebratory shot glasses overflowing with schnapps. I caught up on what everyone was doing while also sharing stories about my new life in the New World.

Before leaving on my trip, I had seriously contemplated coming back to Austria permanently. I had been away for about seven years. But the truth is, when you're homesick, you often romanticize the past and the places you lived. Once you return, once you fall back into the day-to-day grind, it's never quite as rosy as you remembered it.

After a month of vacation in Austria, I prepared to head back to my new home. I knew my mother's heart was going to break, so I acted up and clowned around, and on the day I left there were both laughter and tears.

I said my goodbyes, got into my Parisienne and headed back to France for the transatlantic crossing back to my adopted homeland. Toronto was where my future lay, the place where I would marry and raise a family, the place where I would build my business, block by block, factory by factory, into one of the world's biggest car parts manufacturers.

◇◇◇◇◇

After I returned from Austria, my company continued to grow, and I held on to my best managers by giving them a share of the profits and ownership—the same formula I had worked out with my first manager, Herman Koob. Managers were able to run the factories as their own businesses and they got a portion of the profits, while I was able to harness their entrepreneurial energy and enthusiasm to grow the company.

Most of the toolmakers I hired in those early years were immigrants: Austrians, Germans, Scotsmen, Englishmen—all of them hard-working and, just like me, here to build a better life.

I put in bonus systems to keep my best guys and to spur them on. When I got a contract, I'd say to them, "If you can do it faster, I'll give you a cut." If I had a job for a tool quoted at $5,000, and the total costs were $1,000, that meant we had $4,000 in profits. I laid it all out for them. They could see how much money was on the line and exactly how much more they could make. I never hid anything—it was all out in the open. I said, "This is what you'll get," and they always came through.

By this time, we were building the tools and producing the parts. Back in the early days, bidding was haphazard. Today, the bidding process is very clinical and you have to be an approved supplier. But back then, you might take a buyer or owner out for dinner and get your foot in the door for quoting on jobs down the road.

When we did get a quote, it took us about a day to figure out how to price the tooling and zero in on the cost of the materials. The auto parts business always was and always will be brutally competitive. I could be the cousin of Henry Ford and he couldn't help me land a contract if the price and quality weren't right. Costs are weighed and measured within a fraction of a cent. When you're manufacturing a million pieces, half a cent makes the difference between whether or not you get the contract. You've got to really be on the ball to survive in an environment like that. Our overhead was kept trimmed to the bone, so we always made a profit. Later, we would bid on jobs, even if we knew it meant a small loss, just to prove to customers that we could make a quality product. And once we latched on to a new product line, we rarely ever lost the business.

The early Magna factories all had similar-sounding names: Dieomatic, Unimatic, Multimatic. They sounded modern, automated, machine-like. I made my rounds every week, spending a few hours in each factory. I kept a close eye on the operations, which were fairly small by today's standards. And I knew every single employee.

I showed up to work in a pair of jeans, but I kept a suit handy at the office for the odd customer call or meeting with a banker. Tony Czapka used to rib me: "Hey, Frank, you putting on your monkey suit to go see those fuddy-duddies downtown?"

By the late 1960s, the one-man tool and die shop had grown into a company with five factories, 400 employees and annual sales of approximately $6 million. The Canada–U.S. Auto Pact, signed in 1965, opened up the massive American market to Canadian-based suppliers, and we were soon making and shipping everything from door trim to wheel mouldings and scuff plates to all of the Detroit-based car companies.

More and more of my time was spent in meetings, mapping out product strategies or overcoming engineering issues. The last tool or mould I ever made with my own hands was in 1968. I was no longer just a toolmaker; I was a businessman.

In order to generate even greater growth, I wanted to give every employee a share of the company's profits and ownership. But to do that, the company needed to go public, with shares that traded on the stock market. In 1969, I found the opportunity I had been looking for.

Bill Storey, who was on my board of advisors, introduced me to a shrewd businessman by the name of Jack Warrington. Jack was chairman of Magna Electronics, a publicly traded company that manufactured precision components for the aerospace and defence industries. The defence and aerospace business was highly cyclical and Jack was looking to even out the ups and downs by expanding into other products. On top of that, his company's sales were flat. So he probably figured that by acquiring our company, in an industry that was going gangbusters, he could shore up his business and boost profits. Jack and I hashed out the broad details of a possible merger on a ski lift one Sunday afternoon at a resort north of Toronto. Magna Electronics was doing about $4 to $5 million in annual sales at the time. Our company was doing slightly more. After a few months of back-and-forth negotiating, we did the deal. I got $1 million in cash and shares of Magna Electronics. It was 1969, twelve years after I had started my own business, and I was a millionaire!

Between Burt Pabst and me, we controlled about 40 percent of the company stock. But we were pretty green when it came to how public companies were run. Even though our shareholdings were substantial, and even though we both had a seat on the board, we had no say in the direction of the company. The directors were only interested in spiking the stock price, so they kept pushing the aerospace side of the business, which investors found alluring. Aerospace was the hot technology stock of its day, but it was a money-loser. The way Burt and I saw it, the company was heading in the wrong direction. Everything I had worked to build over the past decade was going down the drain. Because I couldn't sway the board, and because I had no real control, I decided to sell my shares. I was going to start all over again.

I told my fellow board members my intentions, and a number of them asked if I would sell my shares to them. We drew up a contract and they issued a promissory note. But when the note came due, they didn't have the money. I could have tried to collect the money by launching legal action, but I had never sued anybody in my life. Besides, the money wasn't my real interest. My one and only interest was running Magna the way I felt it ought to be run. I had no animosity toward the board members. But I told them that, in lieu of the money they owed me, they would have to resign from the board. From that point forward, I was at the helm; I steered the company. We kept the defence and aerospace business, but the auto industry was where our future lay.

I was now also in a position where I could expand the profit and equity participation plan to include every employee. I felt passionately that if employees had a real and tangible stake in the company's success, they would be more motivated to produce a better product for a better price. I called this profit- and equity-sharing philosophy "Fair Enterprise." It was based on the idea that all of the company's key stakeholders—including society at large—have a moral right to share in the success of the business. Through Fair Enterprise, I set Magna on a course of incredible growth and profitability.

If you want to know what makes Magna tick—what drives the company to be the very best, what fires up our people to work better, harder, smarter—you need to understand what Fair Enterprise is all about.

MAKE YOUR EMPLOYEES PARTNERS IN PROFITS

When I first started out in business, I made my top performers partners in profits and I gave them a share of the ownership. Eventually, when my firm became a publicly traded company, I was able to give every employee the chance to own a portion of the company and to share in the profits. I called this profit-and equity-sharing philosophy "Fair Enterprise." Bottom line: if employees have a real and tangible stake in the company's success, they will be more motivated to produce a better product for a better price.

CHAPTER 3

FAIR ENTERPRISE: GIVING EVERYONE A PIECE OF THE ACTION

What makes people get up in the morning? Basically, people want to make a better life for themselves and their families.

A year after my automotive parts company merged with Magna Electronics and we adopted the new name Magna International, we began sharing profits and ownership with our employees through a profit and equity participation plan. I had always believed that a company could be more productive and more competitive if it was able to harness the driving forces of the business—management, employees and investors—and get them to all pull in the same direction. Or to put it another way: if you have a wagon pulled by three horses, and each of the horses runs off in a different direction, you usually end up in the ditch.

As Magna continued to grow in size, I wanted to entrench the company's Fair Enterprise operating philosophy in a formal document with simple, straightforward principles—

29

something transparent and clearly spelled out, so that everyone knew upfront what their share of the profits was.

That's when I came up with the idea of a Corporate Constitution. It's the cornerstone of our entrepreneurial culture. And the heart of the Corporate Constitution is a clear-cut formula that allows Magna's key stakeholders to participate in the company's growth and profitability.

I believe Magna is the only company in the world with such a constitution. It is an economic covenant or pact between the company's key stakeholders—employees, management, shareholders and society—that predetermines the percentage of annual profits shared by each group.

In 1984, Magna formally adopted its unique Constitution, although we had operated under its core profit-sharing principles for a number of years. I remember when we first drafted the Constitution, one of the corporate lawyers said to me, "Frank, are you crazy? Why would you put this in writing? If you didn't have a Constitution, you could take an even bigger portion of the profits." That's precisely why the Constitution is so important: because its principles are stronger than any one person, including myself, the company founder and, at the time it was written, the controlling shareholder.

Magna's Corporate Constitution has governed the way Magna does business for more than thirty years now. It's published each year in our annual report to shareholders. It hangs on the walls of our offices and factories around the world. And it is engraved into a granite plaque that greets visitors in the lobby of Magna's head office in Aurora, Ontario.

MAGNA'S CORPORATE CONSTITUTION

Employee Equity and Profit Participation

Ten percent of Magna's qualifying profit before tax will be allocated to eligible employees. These funds will be used for the purchase of Magna shares in trust for eligible employees and for cash distributions to eligible employees, recognizing length of service.

Shareholder Profit Participation

Magna will distribute, on average over a three-year period, not less than 20 percent of its annual net profit after tax to shareholders.

Management Profit Participation

To obtain long-term contractual commitment, Magna provides a compensation arrangement to corporate management which allows for base salaries comparable to industry standards, plus incentive bonuses, in total, of up to 6 percent of its profit before tax.

Research and Development

Magna will allocate a minimum of 7 percent of its profit before tax for research and development to ensure its long-term viability.

Social Responsibility

Magna will allocate a maximum of 2 percent of its profit before tax for charitable, cultural, educational and political purposes to support the basic fabric of society.

Unrelated Investments

Magna Common shareholders will have the right to approve any investment in an unrelated business in the event such investment together with all other investments in unrelated businesses exceeds 20 percent of Magna's equity.

Board of Directors

Magna believes that outside directors provide independent counsel and discipline. A majority of the members of Magna's Board of Directors will be outsiders.

Constitutional Amendments

A change to Magna's Corporate Constitution will require the approval of its Common shareholders.

This document is much more than corporate window dressing or a fancy mission statement. The foremost principle of the Constitution is that we predetermine what we do with our annual profits or, as I prefer to say, how we slice up the pie.

Here, in a nutshell, is how it works:

We can't make a profit without workers. Magna's employees design, engineer and manufacture quality products at globally competitive prices. As a result, they pocket 10 percent of the company's annual profit before tax in the form of stock and cash. To determine each employee's share of the profits, we use a formula that rewards loyalty, measured by years of service, and performance, captured by the level of salary.

Magna's investors provide the capital needed to build new factories, purchase new equipment and fund product research, so 20 percent of our profit goes to shareholders in the form of a dividend, a quarterly cash payment tied to every share owned.

In order to run a successful business, you also need good management that can provide the strategic leadership needed to guide long-term growth, so senior management gets 6 percent of the company's annual profit before tax.

The company must develop new products and technologies to remain competitive down the road, so we plow 7 percent of our annual profits into R & D each year.

And reinvestment in the communities where Magna operates makes us a valued employer and a good corporate citizen, so 2 percent of our profit goes to charities and non-profit groups in the communities and countries where our employees live and work. The rest is reinvested and taxed.

MAGNA'S PROFIT-SHARING FORMULA

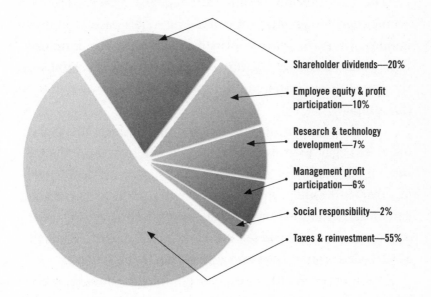

Shareholder dividends—20%

Employee equity & profit participation—10%

Research & technology development—7%

Management profit participation—6%

Social responsibility—2%

Taxes & reinvestment—55%

At the heart of Magna's unique Corporate Constitution is a profit-sharing formula that predetermines how the company's annual profits are divided among its key stakeholders: employees, investors, management and society.

Basically, the Constitution publicly declares and defines the rights of investors, employees, management and society to share in Magna's growth and success, and it includes a number of principles that hold management accountable to employees and shareholders. The Constitution also gives shareholders a number of rights, such as the right to approve significant investments in an unrelated business. The only regret I have regarding the Corporate Constitution is that I didn't include a provision prohibiting the company from going into debt.

I feel Magna was never given due credit for the Constitution over the years. We were talking about stakeholder rights thirty years before the phrase became common business jargon. It was, and still is, a one-of-a-kind business document, a revolutionary way of spelling out the rights and obligations of stakeholders.

The Constitution became our "Magna Carta"—an economic charter of rights that makes everyone a partner in profitability. In 1975, Magna formally established the Employee Equity and Profit Participation Program, which gave employees the opportunity to share in both the profits and ownership of the company.

Our Fair Enterprise approach to doing business was paying off. Sales began to grow at a rapid pace, climbing more than 30 percent per year on average. Magna had started the decade with less than $10 million in sales and several product lines. By the end of the decade, Magna was making approximately 200 different components and had sales of close to $200 million. When the 1980s rolled around, sales and growth shot up even higher.

When I started out in business, I didn't have any grand philosophies—I was simply struggling to get the business off the ground and make enough money to cover my operating and living expenses. What I would later label as the Fair Enterprise philosophy evolved naturally from the way my business grew, such as my making Herman Koob a partner.

I had no financial studies or spreadsheets—I just knew in my gut that if you gave everyone a cut of the action, your business would grow and make more money. I wanted managers and workers to get a portion of the profits and become part owners. There's nothing like ownership to instill pride and create drive and hustle. It's just common sense: when you own a piece of the machine you're working on, and you get a slice of the profits you help produce, you care more, you work harder.

Think about it this way: if you rent an apartment, it's not the same as owning a house. If you invest your own money in buying a house, no matter how small, you will take greater care of it—you will paint the trim, sweep the sidewalks and tend the gardens. It's amazing what ownership does to people. When people own things, their mentality changes. They acquire a whole new outlook.

And because of Fair Enterprise, I believe that Magna is much more than a company. It is a whole new economic culture—something I describe as an organic, industrial genetic formula for growth.

When an acorn falls from an oak tree, the new oak tree that springs up carries the same genetic blueprint. The same principle holds true at Magna. Every single one of our factories is an independent profit centre capable of reproducing itself many times over, much as a cell replicates itself by subdividing over and over again.

Magna's factories, or divisions, are run by entrepreneurial, hands-on managers. When one of these managers starts a new division with a new product, it splits off from the original factory and the manager gets a cut of the profits from both factories. And the same process can repeat itself many times over, until there are enough factories to form a new Magna group specializing in a new product line.

The general manager of a Magna factory always has an assistant general manager, someone who's a strong operator, a real up-and-comer. The formula we established early on was that the general manager gets 3 percent of the factory's profits, while the assistant gets 2 percent. But if the general manager wants to grow and earn more, he has to go out and open a new factory. And when he does that, the assistant becomes the general manager and gets 3 percent of the profits, while the former general manager still gets 2 percent at the original factory he used to run plus 3 percent at the new factory he starts. If a general manager is a really good operator with a knack for making profitable products, he can, over time, develop his own product group comprising many different factories. It's essentially what I did when I made Herman Koob a partner and set him up to run his own factory: I replaced myself, and I did it over and over and over again.

Through Magna's operating philosophy and principles, I've created a blueprint for growth. And any entrepreneurial manager that follows that blueprint and walks in my footsteps is capable of creating their own "Magna" within Magna.

The bigger we grow, the more we try to keep the company small and manageable. The factories are a series of stand-alone operating units linked by a common operating philosophy and governed by Magna's unique Corporate Constitution, and by an Employee's Charter of Rights. Magna's corporate head office, meanwhile, functions more like a bank that specializes in human capital and ensures that the factories are allocated the capital they need to continue growing.

An Organic Industrial Genetic Formula

 Magna Corporate Head Office: The head office is the custodian of the culture.

 Magna Group Management: Group management is responsible for marketing and assisting factory managers in maximizing profits within the Corporate Constitution and the Employee's Charter.

 Magna Factory: Every factory is a separate profit centre.

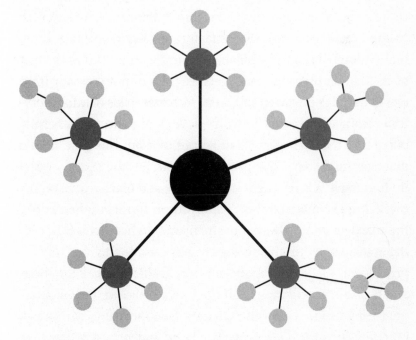

*A good product idea will lead to a new factory,
and a good factory manager can create his own group.*

Our decentralized operating structure allows us to be much more flexible and responsive to the needs of both our customers and our employees. At the same time, the decentralized structure prevents the build-up of bureaucracy, which often chokes the productivity of more traditional, centralized corporations. And by keeping our operating units small and flexible, we're able to foster greater employee involvement and initiative because it's much easier for us to recognize and reward the contributions of individual employees.

We're so decentralized, in fact, that we have no central purchasing department. Instead, we have a head office team that coordinates and negotiates better prices based on the potential volume of Magna's worldwide factories. They then make those high-volume discounts available to our factories. But at the end of the day, it's up to the managers whether or not they buy from one of Magna's preferred suppliers. And that holds true for everything from steel and oil to work gloves and paper clips. If head office told the managers, "You gotta buy from this guy," then a manager might say, "The price was good, but the quality wasn't up to scratch." Or he might say the price and quality were on the mark, but the material wasn't shipped on time. In other words, the manager could always pin the blame on head office. But it's the managers who are ultimately responsible. It's an ironclad principle at Magna: the managers, not head office, call the shots, and they run the divisions as if they were their own businesses.

Competition is another deeply held principle at Magna. Our divisions are so decentralized and independent that they even compete against each other. For example, back in the early 1990s we had one division that made running boards for trucks. Traditionally, this was a metal-stamped component. But one of our plastics divisions began experimenting and came up with a lighter-weight plastic running board that was stronger and cheaper. They captured the business from the other Magna division. Evolution and change are inevitable and relentless: just as the small, stainless steel pieces we made in Magna's early years gave way to aluminum trim and then plastic parts, technological innovations force us to continually change. I always encourage our people to be at the forefront of change rather than play catch-up with the rest of the industry. But when push comes to shove, I would sooner lose business to one of our own product groups than to an outside competitor.

We place all of the day-to-day operating decisions in the hands of our managers, but make them responsible for ensuring profitability, achieving customer satisfaction by shipping quality products on time, and upholding principles such as fair treatment and a safe workplace. When I used to meet with the managers, I would describe their responsibilities in plain language that they all could understand: "Don't screw the employees. Don't screw the shareholders. And if you don't look after your customers, you got no business."

We also tie the pay of our managers to the performance of their factory, which we monitor on an ongoing basis. Because each factory is a separate profit centre, if one starts to lose money, it lights up like a Christmas tree—and we take action to get it back on a path of profitability. And because compensation for plant managers is based on the profitability of their plants, they have to hustle day in and day out. They're always under the gun from the constant pressures and needs of employees, customers and suppliers. So we need to have first-rate incentives to attract and reward good managers. The need for top-notch operators with hands-on experience remains the greatest challenge our company faces as it continues to grow.

At Magna, over the years we've always strived to grow our business, mostly organically, but also through acquisitions. From time to time, however, some of our divisions falter and lose money. When that happens, we use our human capital—the managerial, technical and HR expertise at our disposal—to help bring the division back into the black. At the end of the day, we're builders, not undertakers.

At any given time, there are always some Magna divisions not making a profit. When it comes to new factories, it usually takes time for a start-up to begin making money. Many of our most profitable divisions made very little money or even lost money when they first opened. Other divisions may be facing any number of problems, including a bad manager, technical difficulties or increased competition.

The easy thing to do would be to shut down the divisions that are losing money. But that wouldn't be the right thing to do. We've never been quick to pull the trigger on struggling divisions. Instead, we've always regarded the Magna group of companies as a family—and in a family, you always look out for one another. So we considered it our duty to look after divisions that occasionally ran into problems. In other words, we stood by our factories in the good times and the bad. We preferred to seek a solution in order to preserve jobs for employees, and that requires time and patience. Ultimately, we were much stronger by sticking together. And through this approach we've nursed back to health many divisions that are today generating profits and employing hundreds of people.

Sometimes as management you have no choice—a factory might have a product line that has run its course, or it might have supplied a nearby customer that closed up shop and moved to another location or went out of business. But we at all times tried to avoid closing factories, and even when we did, we made every effort to relocate our employees elsewhere.

Our Fair Enterprise philosophy is why we've grown at a tremendous rate over the past fifty years. And because of our entrepreneurial corporate culture, there is no reason why we cannot continue multiplying and multiplying for many decades to come. There is literally no limit to how big we can become.

In 2007, we celebrated Magna's fiftieth anniversary in business and took some time to reflect on the many milestones and memorable achievements over the years. Despite the significant innovations and technological breakthroughs that had changed our industry, despite the years of record-breaking sales and our expansion into many new countries and continents, the one accomplishment that stood out for me more than any other was this: from the day we first started giving workers "a piece of the action," Magna has shared more than $1 billion in profits with our employees.

In the years ahead, we will share hundreds of millions more. It's part of Magna's unbeatable Fair Enterprise formula for growth.

AVOID BECOMING CENTRALIZED

One of the secrets to Magna's success is its highly decentralized operating structure and entrepreneurial work environment. Decision-making is pushed down to the front lines of the business, where the product is made and where contact with the customer is closest. This decentralized structure prevents bureaucracy and makes the company much more responsive to needs of customers and employees. By keeping your operating units small and flexible, you are better able to create a working environment that fosters employee involvement and recognizes and rewards employee initiative.

CHAPTER 4

MAKE A BETTER PRODUCT
FOR A BETTER PRICE

No government or union can guarantee job security. The best guarantee for job security is having management and employees work together to make a quality product at a competitive price.

The 1970s was when we really started to spread our wings. We began the decade at around $10 million in annual sales. Toward the end, sales had skyrocketed to $180 million, the number of factories mushroomed to more than forty, and we were churning out more than 200 different components.

The Fair Enterprise profit- and stock-sharing plan I had established was generating spectacular growth in sales and profits. But we also had another winning prescription, a can't-fail formula for business success: our strategy of always building a product that was not only better than our competitors' but cheaper as well. I made it our official slogan: *Make a better product for a better price*. And we lived by those words.

My good friend Tony Czapka had become manager of our Unimatic factory in the 1960s. But by the mid-70s, I brought him into the head office, a small, plain brick building located on Wildcat Road in Toronto's northern suburban fringe. My plate was full as a result of all the expansion taking place, and I needed Tony to manage special projects—everything from labour relations to real estate acquisition. He was a jack-of-all-trades, and I could always count on him. What's more, any time there was trouble in one of the plants, Tony sniffed it right away and would take care of it, no questions asked.

Back in the mid-1960s, I had hired a young Austrian tool-maker, Manfred Gingl, who had apprenticed at the same factory in Weiz, Austria, where I learned my trade. Manfred—or Fred, as everyone called him—reminded me a lot of myself ten years earlier. He was a good toolmaker and had a great eye for spotting and seizing new business opportunities. Fred started out in the precision tool room of Speedex Manufacturing, one of Magna's original first four factories, and he quickly rose through the ranks, becoming manager of the factory. By the late 1970s, Fred was put in charge of our entire stamping group and would go on to play a key role in building new product lines for Magna.

It was during this period that we launched a major product diversification strategy—one that would eventually see us produce more than 5,000 different components and systems, a wider array than any parts maker on earth. The company began adding new products such as brackets for mounting motors. Our engineering department grew in size and began tackling the development of bigger, more technically sophisticated products.

At the time, Magna's factories were all clustered in the Toronto area, producing a number of stamped automotive components. We started looking south, to the U.S., to get closer to the Big Three and to sink some roots in the much bigger American market. But we didn't want to set up shop smack in the middle of Motown and lock horns with the unions. Instead, we looked to Iowa, which was relatively close by. In the smaller towns, land was a lot cheaper, the quality of life was better, people worked a little harder, and there were fewer problems. To me, it was economic common sense to locate there.

The first plant we opened in Iowa was in the town of Montezuma, surrounded by lakes and corn fields in the heart of the state. The small towns in Iowa reminded me of the small towns north of Toronto where our original factories were built. By the end of the decade, we had a total of five divisions in Iowa.

One of the main reasons for our growth during that decade is that we were gaining a hard-won identity among the North American automakers as a go-to problem-solver. We had also developed a great reputation for customer service. When the car companies said "Jump," we didn't ask any questions, we only responded, "How high?"

By 1973, the world was in the grips of an oil crisis that drove up the price of fuel, and higher fuel prices forced automakers to find ways of reducing overall vehicle weight in order to achieve better gas mileage. One of the easiest and most effective ways of doing this was by switching from steel to plastic bumpers.

The crisis opened a door for us, and we could see that the industry was moving more and more toward plastic components. In the late 1970s, we acquired some R & D technology from Uniroyal. The company had been working with polyurethane, a material that was pliable and could be easily moulded, and we began experimenting with it. The result of that experimentation was Magna's breakthrough Reaction Injection Moulding

(RIM) process. The new technology led to the establishment of Polyrim, our first plastic bumper operation, located several miles down the road from our family farm. A few years later, Magna's RIM plastic bumpers appeared on Chrysler's famous K-car platform—the vehicle credited with bringing Chrysler back from the brink of bankruptcy. It was the start of Magna's rapid climb to becoming the world's number one supplier of plastic bumpers. By the 1990s, we were pumping out millions of bumpers per year.

Once the Japanese automakers started grabbing market share, the Big Three looked at what they could do to bring down costs. And one of the routes they decided to take was to farm out more production. It was an industry shift that was tailor-made for Magna.

Then in 1978, after several years of R & D work, we hit on something that really made the Big Three sit up and take notice: we pioneered the single-belt, or serpentine, accessory drive system, a game-changer in terms of automotive technology. Our guys took all of the small belts mounted on the front of the engine—belts that were used to drive the alternator, the water pump and the air conditioner—and they created one long belt that snaked its way over top of all of the pulleys. The single-belt accessory drive system required less space than the traditional, multiple-belt system and was ideally suited to the trend at that time toward smaller cars. The Magna single-belt system also offered improved engine efficiency at a lower unit cost—a perfect example of the "make a better product for a better price" formula that would win Magna a bigger and bigger slice of the auto parts market in the decade ahead. A few years later we came up with a revolutionary automatic belt-tensioning device designed to constantly tighten the belt, which lengthens and loosens over time. We weren't just making parts anymore. We were changing the way cars were made.

Automakers began outsourcing more and more components to automotive suppliers—parts that we previously could never bid on because the carmakers manufactured them in-house. These parts included, for the first time, components such as door latches that required a much higher level of engineering and technical expertise, the sort of stuff that simple metal bashers couldn't make. In 1979, Magna opened KTM Locks, our first door latch manufacturing operation. Three years later, we went from being the new kid on the block to becoming one of the largest suppliers of door hinges and door latches to the North American car industry.

It was around this time that we started to grasp our full potential: we could make just about any gear or gizmo under the hood—and more times than not, we could do it better and cheaper than anyone else.

MAKE A BETTER PRODUCT

If you're thinking about starting your own business, consider your personal experiences as a customer. From time to time, we have all experienced the disappointment that comes with buying a bad product or getting poor service. Try to zero in on a business where you think you can make a better product or provide better service, and then focus on that. Do some research and spend a few years working in that business or industry to learn all of the ins and outs.

CHAPTER 5

THE PURSUIT OF ECONOMIC FREEDOM

Human charters of rights alone are not sufficient. They have to be fortified with economic charters of rights. Economic charters of rights will lead to economic democracies, and economic democracies are the basis for democracy itself.

My first up-close look at the fanatical face of totalitarianism came after the Nazis annexed Austria. They introduced into the schools mandatory drills, marching and other shows of allegiance to the state. One time when my class was forced to do some drills, I ducked away and climbed a nearby cherry tree, where I remained safe and out of sight.

I was 12 when the Second World War came to an end. The Nazis, who had occupied and controlled Austria, were in disarray and retreat. The front line of the Russian invasion was only three or four miles from my house. I could hear artillery and gunfire day and night for nearly a month. Everyone could sense the end was coming. We were hoping the English and Americans would arrive before the Russians, but it wasn't to be: the Russians became our new occupiers, and for the next six months they ruled the portion of Austria where we lived.

So within the span of several years, I lived under the two most severe and repressive political systems of the twentieth century: Nazism and Soviet communism. What these totalitarian systems shared in common was a boot on the throat of free expression and individual rights. Under both systems, the individual was subservient to the state. And although I was still very young, I could see that they were incompatible with the human urge to be free.

I believe people everywhere have two basic desires: first, they crave personal freedom, which essentially means they want the right to choose their own road to happiness; and second, they want economic freedom, which means they want to be financially independent. The reality is that people are not truly free unless they have economic freedom. Personal freedom may not mean much to an inner-city kid in Detroit or a single mother in Harlem, for instance. It just means they're free to be hungry and free to be poor.

Even though many people in the West live in highly advanced and prosperous societies, only perhaps 5 percent of the population can be considered economically free. And yet what fuelled me as a young man was the desire to attain economic freedom. It was my fire in the belly, my key motivation in working as hard as I did to build Magna.

Societies in the West have focused on creating great charters of human rights and freedoms, and these rights and freedoms should always be safeguarded—they have laid the groundwork for the development of prosperous, democratic societies. But at the same time, I find it incomprehensible that we as a society do not place a greater emphasis on how people can achieve economic freedom.

Economic freedom has different meanings in different parts of the world. Here in the West, economic freedom would entail accumulating a sufficient amount of wealth after having worked for twenty or so years that you could own a modest home and have enough money in the bank that you could stop working and live off the interest on your savings. You would be free to paint or travel or pursue other hobbies and passions. Yet so very few of us are able to do that. Why?

Societies throughout the ages have developed various economic systems—everything from colonial imperialism to free market trading—as a way to generate the greatest amount of wealth possible. In the past century alone, our world has been governed by three main socio-economic systems, all of which still exist in one form or another: totalitarianism; state enterprise, or socialism; and free enterprise.

Each of these systems has a major flaw. Under a totalitarian economic system, human rights are trampled and economic development is directed by military force, with the result that economic benefits are shared by relatively few people. Under the state enterprise/socialist system, the little wealth that is produced is distributed by state bureaucrats, which eventually leads to an enormous build-up of bureaucracy. The problem with the free enterprise system is that, although it is extremely efficient at creating wealth, greed is not curtailed, and as a result more and more capital becomes concentrated in the hands of fewer and fewer people. What's more, the democratic system within a free enterprise society is vote-driven. In practical terms, this means that political parties cater to the masses by introducing wealth redistribution measures and socialistic programs. The inevitable result is that the free enterprise system gets slowly pulled toward the state enterprise/socialist economic system, where the state takes and distributes a larger and larger portion of the wealth.

I believe that we must do everything possible to preserve the free enterprise system. Without free enterprise, there is no free society. Yet I also realize that, from time to time, the free enterprise system can be self-destructive, especially when it is in the grip of unbridled greed. The financial meltdown triggered by Wall Street in 2008 is an unforgettable example.

The real dilemma confronting all three systems is the creation of wealth and its distribution. The state enterprise/socialist system is effective at distributing wealth, but it stifles productivity and wealth creation. Free enterprise, on the other hand, is effective at creating wealth, but the concentration of capital in the hands of relatively few people leads to increased taxation and social programs designed to redistribute wealth on a more even basis—what we see in Europe today and increasingly in North America. We have become so absorbed with distributing wealth that we have neglected ensuring that we have the right environment to create wealth.

There is another option. It's the system we practice at Magna called Fair Enterprise. It's an economic philosophy or system that recognizes that a successful business is driven by three forces: managers, workers and investors, and that all three driving forces have a moral right to share in the success of the business. When workers get a percentage of the profits, when they feel they have something at stake, then they work harder and think smarter, and that makes a business faster, stronger, more competitive. The state doesn't have the right to tell a business what it should do with its profits, but via tax incentives it can encourage more businesses to adopt a Fair Enterprise system.

Economic Systems

Fair enterprise is designed to prevent the free enterprise system from being pulled toward the state enterprise system

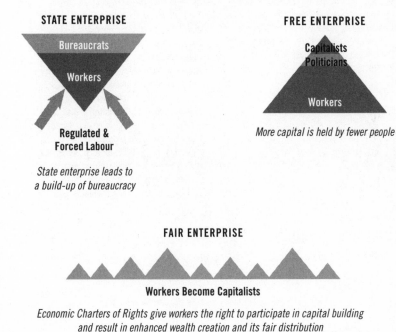

STATE ENTERPRISE

Bureaucrats

Workers

Regulated & Forced Labour

State enterprise leads to a build-up of bureaucracy

FREE ENTERPRISE

Capitalists
Politicians

Workers

More capital is held by fewer people

FAIR ENTERPRISE

Workers Become Capitalists

Economic Charters of Rights give workers the right to participate in capital building and result in enhanced wealth creation and its fair distribution

Economic Systems (A Condensed Summary)

Totalitarian System or Dictatorship

State Enterprise/ Socialist System

Suppressing human rights and freedoms

Making the individual subservient to the state

Throughout history there have been many kinds of dictators, from kings and military generals to Hitler and Stalin. In a totalitarian system there is little or no concern for human rights, and relatively few people benefit economically. Those few tell the rest of the people what is good for them at the point of a gun. Totalitarian systems inevitably fail because they are incompatible with the human spirit, and they attempt to suppress the human desire for personal and economic freedom.

The state enterprise, or socialist, system is based on the philosophy that wealth should be redistributed so that there are not great differences in income levels. Consequently, there is not enough incentive for individuals to create more wealth by working harder and by being more innovative and productive. The little wealth that is created is distributed by state bureaucrats, and the harder bureaucrats work, the more bureaucrats they create. This leads to an enormous build-up of bureaucracy, which in turn chokes the productive juices of society and stifles individual ingenuity and innovation. State enterprise also results in the collectivization of individuals, and more and more people become dependent on the state for their existence. History has proven that state enterprise systems always fail, leading to greater poverty and lower living standards.

Free Enterprise System

Fair Enterprise System

**Creating the foundation
of a free society**

**Creating capitalists
out of workers**

Free enterprise is extremely effective at creating wealth, but its major flaw is that more and more capital ends up being held by fewer and fewer people. This in turn leads to more state intervention and calls for greater redistribution of wealth. The free enterprise system is based on a democratic charter of rights and freedoms, which guarantees, among other things, the right to vote. This means that the system is constituency-driven. If politicians don't cater to the masses, they won't get elected. As a result, politicians promise more and more socialistic economic programs in order to win elected office. The free enterprise system therefore gets pulled toward state enterprise.

In order for free enterprise to avoid being absorbed by state enterprise, businesses must create more capitalists* by sharing profits and equity with workers so they can accumulate capital.

A capitalist is an individual who works hard to accumulate enough capital to become economically independent and who wants to pay taxes to a state with a lean, efficient government that respects the rights and freedoms of individuals and maintains basic laws and regulations in regard to safety, health, education and the environment, while helping people who, for one reason or another, cannot look after themselves.

The fair enterprise system is an alternative to the state enterprise and free enterprise systems. Its philosophy is based upon the principle that people desire economic freedom as well as individual freedom. Via tax incentives, however, businesses can be encouraged to adopt an economic charter of rights, which gives workers the right to participate in capital building. Economic charters of rights will lead to economic democracies, and economic democracies are the basis for democracy itself.

55

The Fair Enterprise system is designed to generate greater wealth, and then distribute that wealth in a way that is much fairer and more broadly based than any other system. The creation and distribution of wealth is at the crux of any economic system. And every economic system must answer two fundamental questions: How do you create wealth? And who gets the wealth? Fair Enterprise recognizes that if you don't create wealth in the first place, there's nothing to distribute. It further recognizes that the people who create wealth should all get a fair share of that wealth. Rather than pit workers against capitalists, Fair Enterprise turns workers into capitalists. The Fair Enterprise system is a safety valve, or buffer, designed to prevent free enterprise from being dragged toward state enterprise.

Unfortunately, the history of mankind has always been, and still is, dominated by the Golden Rule: the man who has the gold makes the rules. Centuries ago, you knew who the guy with the gold was—it was the king up on the hill in his castle. But today, no one knows who the kings are—they live in penthouse condominiums in Manhattan and beach homes in Malibu. And these kings own most of the world's wealth at a time when the gap between the rich and the lower and middle classes is growing larger and larger.

I would never want anyone to dominate me or my children, and if I feel that strongly, then I should never expect to be able to dominate anyone else. So the challenge we as a society face is this: we must find a way to dismantle the chains of domination—not via a destructive revolution, but via a revolution of the mind. We've built great political democracies, but we still haven't attained economic democracies.

And this fact goes to the heart of what Fair Enterprise is all about. The core philosophy behind Fair Enterprise is that our human charters of rights need to be augmented and fortified with economic charters of rights, including the right of workers to accumulate wealth through equity and profit participation. Economic charters of rights will lay the foundation for economic democracies, and economic democracies are the basis for democracy itself.

In a Fair Enterprise system, a business would have an economic charter of rights, its employees would get a portion of the profits and ownership in the company, and most of the company's profits would be reinvested in the country. If businesses operating under Fair Enterprise principles paid a lower tax rate, more businesses would adopt these principles, and more employees would begin to reap the benefits of having a financial stake in their place of employment. Businesses, meanwhile, would become more competitive. A country adopting such a system would see an increase in productivity and a much fairer and broader-based distribution of wealth than any system that has previously existed. In short, the country would blossom economically.

I truly believe that Fair Enterprise, more than any other system, would give the greatest number of citizens the opportunity to achieve economic freedom—one of the great longings of individuals everywhere.

Fair Enterprise worked for my company. It can work for your company too. And if more and more companies adopted it, I believe it could work for entire countries, igniting economic growth and development on a scale never before seen.

KEEP YOUR WORD

If you make a commitment, make sure you can live up to it. When you're a manager, you have to work hard to win the trust and respect of your employees. You can always find new business if you lose a customer, but if you tarnish your reputation, it is very difficult to regain. And when it comes to trust, there are no shortcuts or detours—once you've lost that trust, you can never get it back.

CHAPTER 6

STANDING IN THE WINNER'S CIRCLE

Success in life can only be measured by the degree of happiness you reach. But let me tell you, in my experience, it's a lot easier to be happy if you have some money.

My first horse was not much to look at: a bony old grey mare that a Russian soldier gave me.

I was 12 years old, and Russian soldiers were pouring into the foothills of the Austrian Alps during the dying days of the Second World War. Like many of the boys in town, I went into the streets to watch the soldiers, trucks and tanks coming into our village. There were stories going around that some women had been raped, so earlier that morning my mother took a pair of scissors and chopped off my sister Elizabeth's hair and dressed her in a pair of pants to make her look like a boy. And although my mother warned me to stay out of sight, my curiosity got the better of me.

Later in the day, I was standing by a broken-down army truck that had been abandoned at the side of the road when a Russian soldier rode by on horseback, while another solider walked behind him on foot. He got off the horse and immediately went to work trying to fix the truck. Once he got the engine started, he started laughing and shouting, but before taking off he handed me the reins of his horse.

There I was, just a barefoot schoolboy—the proud owner of my own horse! I knew a farm nearby that had an abandoned shed, and I brought her over and set her up in a makeshift stall. The next morning, I bolted out of bed and ran over to the shed to see my horse. I petted her, talked to her and fed her from my hand. A day later, I arrived at the shed early in the morning and found the door open and the stall empty. My heart sank. I wanted to believe that she had run away. But as the war dragged on, food was becoming scarcer, and my horse had probably been taken away in the middle of the night and butchered.

I'm a great believer that experiences in life help shape our character and our destiny—they are the ingredients that make us who we are. That brief experience with the horse ignited in me a passion that remains to this day.

Horses are such noble creatures. They're elegant and beautiful but at the same time they also have an incredible, primitive power, stamina and courage. They've played a great role in the civilization of mankind, from farming and warfare to opening up new continents. If there were no horses in the world, there would definitely be something missing.

Horses are also a great equalizer. For me, they provide a counterbalance to the mechanized and industrialized world of automotive manufacturing, where metal gears and plastic parts can be weighed and measured and calibrated. You can figure out exactly what you're dealing with, right down to a fraction of a millimetre. If something's not right on the production line, you can always stop the machines and reconfigure them. In business, it's beneficial to have an activity that provides a counter-balance—a release from the sometimes intense and grinding pressure of meeting deadlines, doing deals and poring over financial details.

Horses provide that outlet for me. They're natural, organic, wild—as unpredictable and complex as humans. You have to get to know them, get close to them, read their character, sense their mood and develop a feel for their personality. On any given day, a horse might be anxious or playful, fearful or curious. But that very unpredictability is what makes horses so exhilarating.

One of the places I thoroughly enjoy is my horse farm in Bourbon County, Kentucky. It's true bluegrass country, known the world over for its stud farms and its whiskies. My preferred time of year to go there is spring. It's lush and green with rolling fields as far as the eye can see. In the cool, early hours of the morning, when the sun is coming up and the fog is still hanging over the blue-tinted grass, it has an almost mystical feel. Spending a few days there, watching the stallions racing through the fields, recharges my mind and my body, and I always leave my Kentucky farm feeling completely reinvigorated.

I bought my first horse in 1961, not long after my business began to take off. It was a riding horse named Tanjo, and I paid around 300 bucks for him. I had him stabled at a farm in Richmond Hill, north of Toronto, close to the first factory we built after outgrowing the old gatehouse where I started Magna. During those early years I worked so many hours that I thought it would be nice to have a horse and be able to ride out into the sunset like Gary Cooper in some old western movie. A few years later, I bought a 150-acre farm in a small country town, and I built a barn for our horse myself, sawing the barn boards by hand and putting up the fencing. After work, during the long, hot evenings of summer, I would often ride my horse through the fields, with the sun sinking behind the trees—exactly how I always imagined it would be. When I sometimes rode Tanjo too hard or too fast, he would make a sharp right turn and head for the woods, knocking me to the ground as he bolted under the branches and foliage.

I got involved in horse racing when the farmer who sold me my first horse asked me one day to join him for an afternoon at the racetrack. Ever since then I've been hooked on the "sport of kings." I was fascinated by every element—the people from all walks of life betting on the horses, the heart-pounding race to the finish line, the anticipation and the thrill of wagering on the outcome of the race. Most of all, it was the challenge involved—the challenge of breeding and training a living creature and then harnessing its raw power and speed to make it a champion.

Spending a Sunday afternoon at the racetrack is great fun. Where else can you have a meal, watch live entertainment and go home with more money in your pocket than you came with? You meet a lot of colourful characters there—everyone from movie stars and rich matrons with their exotic hats to old-school bettors smoking cigars and scrutinizing the racing form the way a stock analyst reads a company's balance sheet. You see people from the highest echelons of wealth and power and people living on the bottom rungs. The one thing that unites them all is the love of horses. They're all there for "the show"—the live spectacle of thoroughbred horse racing.

When the gates explode open, you can feel the ground tremble as the 1,500-pound horses thrust forward, thundering down the dirt track at speeds of thirty-five miles per hour. Thoroughbred horses are the most majestic, powerful athletes on earth, and the intense action of a race—with a bit of prize money riding on the outcome—is one of the most electrifying sporting events you can watch.

Horse racing may be my labour of love, but it's also a tough, sometimes cutthroat business that demands as much skill and savvy as any other financial enterprise. No one can say I haven't paid my dues during the nearly fifty years I've been in the horse racing business. I've mucked out stalls and helped birth many a foal. I can run my hand down a horse's knee or ankle and know right away if it's been shod right. In my earlier years, I spent many nights in the brood mare barn waiting for the brood mare to foal, or give birth to her young. I can tell you what type of grains or grasses my horses are fed, and even where they were grown. There is no aspect of the business that I consider too trivial to manage or oversee. Most times at the track, you're more likely to find me talking to a trainer or a horse groom than drinking a Chardonnay up in the ritzy turf club. It's really no different from any other business: you start at the bottom and you learn the inner workings over time. Even though I've climbed my way to the top of the industry and become one of the world's leading owners and breeders, in my mind I will always be a horseman first and foremost.

Horse racing and breeding has always been a family affair in our household, and it has brought us a lot of enjoyment over the years, a lot of time shared together. My wife, Elfriede, has a hand in virtually all aspects of the business, and often accompanies me to the winner's circle after one of our horses finishes first. As the linchpin who holds our family together, she not only has rock-solid common sense, but she also has great horse sense. My son, Andy, is a wizard when it comes to bloodlines and pedigree. He selects the yearlings and the brood mares and basically matches up the horses that will give us the best chance of siring a champion. But breeding is not an exact science—there's a lot of gut instinct involved.

When Andy was a kid, he would "hot walk" the horses early in the morning after their workout. The horses had to be cooled down and he would take them by the harness and walk them around the barns. While walking the stallions and fillies he would talk to the people who work with the horses, so he got a real feel for the business from the ground up. He would read pedigrees of horses the way some boys study the scoring statistics of their favourite hockey or baseball players. Today, Andy can trace a horse's bloodlines back six generations, and he can do that off the top of his head with probably a few thousand horses.

Our family stable, Adena Springs, has had the good fortune to become one of the world's top thoroughbred horse owners and breeders. But it took years and years of work, a lot of planning and patience, and more than a few setbacks along the way. We've been the leading owners in North America a number of times. Some years our stable has earned more than $10 million in purses. But all the money in the world couldn't buy your stable the top-earner crown—you've got to have the smarts and the know-how, the right team and the right environment. And, like anything in life, luck plays a role.

As an owner, my one overriding goal is simple and straightforward: to breed and develop an extraordinary horse, the kind that comes along once in a lifetime, one whose name will live on for generations. That's what drives me.

My first thoroughbred was a horse named Miss Scooter, a chestnut-coloured filly that cost $700. She won a couple of cheap claiming races and the money from those purses went toward buying additional horses so I could start building up my own stable. I've always believed that great horses carry great names—names that are unique, grab hold of your imagination and stick in your mind: Macho Uno, Awesome Again, Red Bullet, Perfect Sting, Glorious Song. More times than not, my horses have lived up to their billing.

The late 1990s were magical years for our stable. Our horse Touch Gold won the 1997 Belmont Stakes, the last leg of the Triple Crown. Touch Gold had some Northern Dancer blood in him, and he upset Silver Charm, a fan favourite that looked to be a lock on becoming the first Triple Crown winner since Secretariat. Winning the Belmont Stakes was a terrific feeling—a photographer captured the look of joy and triumph in a photo of me punching the air in victory.

The next year, another of our horses, Awesome Again, won the $5.1 million Breeders' Cup Classic at Churchill Downs. It was, at the time, the richest stakes race ever run. The Breeders' Cup Classic is known as the Super Bowl of thoroughbred horse racing—the best of the best. But this particular race in November 1998 is still considered by many in the sport to be the strongest field of all-star horses ever assembled—virtually every horse in the race was a proven winner, a fierce competitor. When you listen to a recording of the track announcer calling the race, shouting uncontrollably as Awesome Again bolts up the middle to grab the lead just before the finish line, it makes the hair on the back of your neck stand up.

I had five horses running on the day that Awesome Again captured the Breeders' Cup Classic. The weather was grey and rainy, and all of my horses in the races leading up to the Cup Classic were finishing poorly. I just figured it wasn't my lucky day. When the Cup Classic race finally came, grooms led the horses to the saddling area. The place was crammed with racing fans and bettors jostling to get an up-close look at the horses, trying to glean some scrap of information that you couldn't get in the racing form: a look of fear or hesitancy in the horse's eye, the head cocked too high or a short, choppy gait. I made my way through the crowd, craning my neck to see for myself how Awesome Again was holding up before the big race. And it was right at that moment when I inadvertently stepped in a big pile of horseshit. When that happens in this business, it's a sure sign that you're lucky. So after having spent the day watching all of my horses lose race after race, I suddenly started feeling a lot better. And sure enough, Lady Luck was on my side: Awesome Again wove through the pack and surged across the finish line, winning one of the most unforgettable races in horse racing history. The track was sloppy and Awesome Again was covered in muck. But on that magnificent day, with shit on my shoes and mud splattered all over my suit, I didn't mind grabbing my horse by the reins and leading him to the winner's circle. It was one of the greatest moments in my horse racing career.

The year before, Awesome Again had also won the Queen's Plate, the oldest stakes race in North America, and Her Majesty Queen Elizabeth II herself presented me with the gold trophy. I knew there was a possibility that I would greet the Queen in person, so I asked Bill Davis, a former Ontario premier and one of Magna's directors, for some pointers on how to behave in the company of a monarch. When Bill finished, I said, "So I shouldn't give her a tap on the bum?" He turned white and said, "Are you crazy?" A number of years later, the Queen visited me at my farm in Kentucky. When she arrived, she got out of her car, extended a hand and said, "It's very nice to see you again." We spent half an hour together. I showed her my stallions and we had a long and detailed discussion about our shared interest in thoroughbred bloodlines. As it turns out, my stable ended up mating one of our promising mares with one of the royal studs, the superb English stallion Motivator. When she left, I wished Her Majesty well. She's got incredible horse sense, and she's a great and gracious lady.

Awesome Again ran in a lot of tough races, and never lost once during that entire year. From the moment I saw him and gave him his name, I felt he had greatness in him. Around the time that Awesome Again was born, Magna had gotten back on its feet after a brush with bankruptcy and was starting to make tremendous strides. The company was setting new sales records and expanding rapidly into Europe. Magna had become "awesome again," and so, in hindsight, it was fitting that I had given that name to a horse that had all the markings of a great champion.

One of our best horses over the last few years—perhaps our greatest horse ever in terms of pure talent and power—was Ghostzapper, the son of Awesome Again. He went undefeated in 2004 and again in 2005 and, like his dad, he won the Breeders' Cup Classic. After he won the race, a number of reporters asked me about the meaning behind his name. I knew the Cup Classic was going to take place close to Halloween, and it got me thinking about ghosts, so Ghostzapper struck me as a perfect name. He could sprint or go a long distance. He could come from behind or take a commanding lead. And unlike his dad, who was not physically striking, Ghostzapper was an intimidating presence at the track, with a powerful physique and muscles that bulged beneath his sleek coat. He destroyed most of his opponents. No horse in the history of the world has been clocked at a faster speed.

But the thoroughbred racehorse I will always love best— the horse I will never forget—is Glorious Song. She was a small brown filly with a shaggy black mane that made her look like a bear. She was blessed with the bloodlines of a champion, but it was her character and charisma that drew me to her. She had a look in her eyes and a stillness about her, the sort of quiet confidence that you often see in some of the truly great horses. Although she was born and bred to be in the winner's circle, no one thought much of her, and she was put up for auction at a yearling sale in 1977. I bought her for what turned out to be the garage-sale price of $36,000. She would go on to become the first Canadian thoroughbred to ever earn more than $1 million in prize winnings.

When Glorious Song ran at age two, she was so impressive that Texas billionaire oilman Nelson Bunker Hunt purchased a half-interest in her for $500,000—money that I plowed back into our stable. Slender and long-limbed, Glorious Song beat some of the top male horses on the continent. I remember taking her down to the Santa Margarita Handicap in Los Angeles as a four-year-old, and a number of the Californians were shaking their head at this wild-looking, long-haired Canadian horse that had come from way up north to challenge the top mares on the west coast. When the race started, Glorious Song exploded out of the gate and won convincingly. In 1980, she received the Eclipse Award for outstanding filly and mare—considered the Oscars of the thoroughbred horse world. She is still regarded as one of the greatest thoroughbreds Canada has ever produced.

But on a fall day back in 1980, I reluctantly sold that champion with the heart of a lion for $1 million. It was a huge blow to me. I had found and developed a truly special horse—one of the greats—and I had to let her go.

> **KNOW YOUR BUSINESS INSIDE OUT**
> *When you run your own business, you've got to know the business inside out. You've got to have a firm handle on all aspects of the operation, right down to knowing where the supplies are stored and when the garbage gets picked up. Because when you start overlooking the smaller details, that's when things begin to fall through the cracks and problems begin to snowball.*

CHAPTER 7

THE BOARDROOM REVOLT

If someone tells me, "Frank, I'm a friend of yours," I always say, "That's nice to hear, but you don't have to tell me—prove it."

I t had taken me years to build up my stable, but I had no choice: I had to sell Glorious Song and many of my best thoroughbreds to begin stockpiling cash for a looming boardroom battle. Several members of the Magna board wanted to push me out, and I needed to quickly raise cash to buy up Magna shares in order to prevent a hostile takeover. I loved my horses, but the business I had built meant more to me than anything. To prepare for the showdown, I sold off a sizeable portion of my stable, liquidated my million-dollar interest in Glorious Song, and with the cash I began buying up Magna shares on the open market. I was not going to lose Magna, even if it cost me that magnificent horse.

Interest rates were going through the roof back then—they were close to 20 percent, causing many people to lose their homes—so I had to be careful about how much money

I borrowed from the banks. My only other option was to sell my most valuable horses. In my desperation to raise cash, I practically gave Glorious Song away. She fetched $6 million three years after I sold her. Although she wasn't a horse I had bred from infancy, I had purchased her when she was just a yearling and developed her into a champion, one of the most celebrated horses to ever come out of Canada. It devastated me to lose her. But Magna—that was my life. That was the foundation of my economic freedom. And I wasn't going to lose Magna.

The attempted boardroom coup had taken me completely by surprise. I felt as if I had been knifed in the back. I owned about 30 percent of the Magna shares, but I didn't have complete control of the company. Some of the senior directors knew that there was a rift between the president, Helmut Hofmann, and me over the direction of the company. I wanted to decentralize the company. We were growing into a traditional type of corporate structure, with one president and everyone underneath reporting to him. One big pyramid. It wasn't the Magna way. When you're centralized and things go wrong, it's harder to find the problems, tougher to spot the leaks and cracks. But by decentralizing, you bring everything out of the closet. Hofmann was a great operations guy, and I wanted him to turn around our aerospace and defence division, the old Magna Electronics, which was floundering and starting to drag down our profits.

So with the rift out in full view, some directors smelled an opportunity to drive a wedge in and seize control. George Gardiner, one of the directors who was orchestrating the coup, stood up and said, "I've got a lot of money invested here, and I don't think the company is being run properly. We think we should have a different CEO." He levelled a number of accusations against me, including misappropriation of funds concerning nickel-and-dime stuff like taxi fares and lunch expenses, a charge that was later proved to be unfounded. And he concluded by saying that I was no longer the best man to run the company.

Looking back, I was still a little wet behind the ears when it came to boardroom politics, and I didn't see the coup brewing. It was underhanded. I believe it was hatched to gain control by removing me from the company. The directors lined up against me were not builders; a few of them were savvy and experienced stock players who had flipped companies and engineered takeovers. With me out of the way, investors and competitors might have thought the company was in play. Larger multinationals on the prowl for assets would likely have swooped in and swallowed us up. But in the process, the share price would have climbed, producing a juicy profit.

Business is business, but I took this personally. I was bleeding inside. I said to them, "You sons of bitches, you didn't even have the guts to confront me in person before the meeting. This is bullshit. I'm going to fight you and I'm going to remove you from the board. I guarantee you that." And then I walked out of the boardroom.

I was always a good toolmaker, a good auto parts maker, but when it came down to the finer side of business, the fancy business bylaws and arcane stock exchange regulations, I was out of my element, so I had to learn quickly what manoeuvres I had at my disposal. I knew I had the support of the employees and the managers—they were guys like me, toolmakers and factory workers from small towns like Weiz. And I knew I had the support of a number of directors, including Tony Czapka and Burt Pabst—both sizeable shareholders and trusted friends who were with me in the early days when we worked through the night together to meet a deadline and then ran boxes of metal parts over to General Motors in my beat-up Chevy.

Perhaps the rebellious directors thought I would walk away from the fight; if they did, they underestimated me. There was no way I was going to lose the company that I had built over the past twenty years through sheer sacrifice, sweat and hustle. For the directors, Magna was just one of their many investments. For me, it was my whole life: I had poured all of my savings, all of my heart into that company.

As a young man I had vowed that I would never crawl from anyone, and if some of the directors thought they were going to take the company from me without a fight, they were dead wrong. I crushed the boardroom revolt and brought in some new board members. I won the battle, but I paid a heavy price, financially and emotionally, and I learned a valuable lesson. I vowed from that day on that I would have 60 percent of the voting control. I kept buying up shares on the market until I owned a clear majority of Magna's shares. I swore I was never going to let that kind of close call happen again.

It was the first time I came close to losing everything I had worked so hard to build. But there would come another time, and it would be much worse.

BE TRANSPARENT

A business or any organization functions best when everything is transparent. Workers are very smart: if they know management is not straight up or is hiding something, you will never be able to win their hearts. When I had my first factory, I would sit with the employees during lunch and show them the company bank book. I had always promised myself that when I ran my own business, everything would be upfront and out in the open. That's why at Magna I created an operating philosophy that included open books and open doors.

CHAPTER 8

UNHAPPINESS IS CONTAGIOUS

Unhappiness is contagious, and when you have unhappy employees, there's no way you can make a quality product at a competitive price.

Whenever I walk into any Magna factory in any corner of the world, I don't have to look at the balance sheet to know if it is making money or not: all I have to do is look at the employees' faces. If the employees are happy, then I know the factory is a money-maker. If the employees don't look happy, odds are pretty good the factory is losing money.

I've always maintained that unfairness in the workplace leads to unhappiness, and unhappiness is contagious. When you have disgruntled employees and unhappiness spreading through the workplace, there's no way a business can make quality products at a competitive price.

As my business grew, I wanted to avoid the traditional automotive factory environment with punch clocks and massive factories with thousands of employees who became nameless and faceless numbers. I wanted to recreate the environment that existed in the original tool shop that I started back in 1957, when I knew every employee and we would have lunch together. It was there, sitting at the table with our brown paper bags and lunch pails, that we would most often solve a quality problem or kick around ideas for speeding up the production line. I wanted to create a workplace that fostered open communication between management and employees, a place where individual initiative could be recognized and rewarded.

This is easier to do when the business is small; once you start growing and you've got thousands of employees, you need to start putting systems in place. I had developed a decentralized, entrepreneurial operating system that drove our profits and I had devised a formula and a system for sharing those profits. But my next challenge was something just as important: to come up with a system for ensuring the fair treatment of our employees.

So in 1988, with a growing number of operating divisions located throughout North America and Europe, I created an Employee's Charter. It was built around the long-standing principles of fairness and concern for people that were the hallmark of Magna's employee relations philosophy, and it spelled out, for the first time, a framework for fairness in the workplace.

The Charter guarantees every Magna employee a number of fundamental rights, including fair treatment, a safe and healthful workplace, and competitive wages and benefits. One of the key Charter principles, the right of Employee Equity and Profit Participation, had previously been enshrined in Magna's Corporate Constitution and had already been put into practice at Magna for several decades. And because I had personally experienced discrimination and unfairness as an employee, I made Fair Treatment another key principle of the Charter.

MAGNA INTERNATIONAL INC.
EMPLOYEE'S CHARTER

Magna is committed to an operating philosophy which is based on fairness and concern for people. This philosophy is part of Magna's Fair Enterprise culture in which employees and management share in the responsibility to ensure the success of the company. It includes these principles:

Job Security

Being competitive by making a better product for a better price is the best way to enhance job security. Magna is committed to working together with you to help protect your job security.

To assist you, Magna will provide:
- Job Counselling
- Training
- Employee Assistance Programs

A Safe and Healthful Workplace

Magna strives to provide you with a working environment which is safe and healthful.

Fair Treatment

Magna offers equal opportunities based on an individual's qualifications and performance, free from discrimination or favouritism.

Competitive Wages and Benefits

Magna will provide you with information which will enable you to compare your total compensation, including total wages and total benefits, with those earned by employees of your competitors, as well as with other plants in your community. If your total compensation is found not to be competitive, then your wages will be adjusted.

Employee Equity and Profit Participation

Magna believes that every employee should share in the financial success of the company.

Communication and Information

Through regular monthly meetings between management and employees and through publications, Magna will provide you with information so that you will know what is going on in your company and within the industry.

The Hotline

Should you have a problem, or feel the above principles are not being met, we encourage you to call the Hotline or use the self-addressed Hotline Envelopes to register your complaints. You do not have to give your name, but if you do, it will be held in strict confidence. Hotline Investigators will answer your call. The Hotline is committed to investigate and resolve all concerns or complaints and must report the outcome to Magna's Global Human Resources Department.

Employee Relations Advisory Board

The Employee Relations Advisory Board is a group of people who have proven recognition and credibility relating to humanitarian and social issues. This Board will monitor, advise and ensure that Magna operates within the spirit of the Magna Employee's Charter and the principles of Magna's Corporate Constitution.

The Magna system is built on merit and rewarding individuals according to their input and initiative, without regard to an employee's race or gender or cultural background. At Magna, we will never tolerate discrimination—it's not only unethical, it's simply bad business.

Magna had established an Employee Hotline a few years earlier for any employee who wanted to report a concern or problem. I made the hotline a key part of the Employee's Charter, so that employees could confidentially call a toll-free number if they had a problem or if they believed any of their rights had been violated. The hotline was basically a built-in mechanism for ensuring that the Charter was being upheld. I hand-picked the first hotline investigators—employees right off the factory floor who knew the sorts of workplace issues that could crop up while working on an assembly line.

Our hotline investigated everything from sudden terminations to allegations of sexual harassment involving supervisors and line workers to fist fights on the factory floor and managers smoking in their office in violation of a no-smoking policy in the workplace.

The Charter is posted in every single division around the world and printed in more than twenty different languages, reflecting the multicultural diversity of Magna's workforce. In much the same way that Magna's Corporate Constitution is a blueprint for the company's growth and success, the Employee's Charter and our employee relations programs have provided a framework for ensuring fairness in the workplace.

We want to run a fair ship, but in order to do that, we need to know directly from our employees whether or not they are being treated with fairness and dignity. Employees are smart: they know what's right and what's fair. So giving employees a voice is the best formula for ensuring fairness and success. If there are problems in the workplace, we provide employees with a number of ways to let us know about them so that we can flush out anything that isn't right or fair. The most important tool for rooting out problems is the annual Employee Opinion Survey, which we established at all of the company's divisions soon after implementing the Employee's Charter. The survey gauges the temperature of the factory by listening to the opinions of our employees and getting the pulse of how they feel. It has become a vital tool for measuring how well Magna's divisions are living up to the principles of the Employee's Charter.

After I introduced the Employee Opinion Survey, one of the managers asked, "What are you doing, Frank? Spying on us?" Another manager was so angered by it that when the employee newsletter announcing the new survey arrived at the factory, he took the bundles of newsprint and, standing on the loading dock in full view of the employees, hurled them into a big metal waste bin. He was one of our top managers, tough but fair. The employees respected him. But it wasn't him that I was worried about. It was all the new managers who had been hired during the boom years of the 1980s when we were opening new factories every other month. Most of these new managers hadn't been immersed in the Magna culture, they didn't come up through the ranks. Some of them just paid lip service to our Fair Enterprise culture but didn't really live it. So if there was unfairness, or if employees were being treated poorly, the survey would flush it out, and we would remove the bad managers. In future years, when we started growing globally, we created a management training program specifically designed to instill the Magna culture in our new managers, so that the Fair Enterprise principles would run through their veins. We called it "Magna-tizing" them.

Because employees are partners in Magna's profitability, I believe they should have a say in how the company was run. When workers are given a voice in running the business—when there is greater democracy in the workplace—it is much easier to make a better product for a better price.

In the early 1990s, I established a new mechanism for resolving disputes at the divisional level—one that placed a greater amount of decision-making power in the hands of employees. Fairness Committees became an important vehicle for helping to clear up misunderstandings and resolve problems within a division. Fairness Committees were employee democracy in action. Composed of up to five volunteers, from rank-and-file employees to managerial staff, the committees could—and sometimes did—overturn management decisions.

A few years later, I introduced another tool of employee democracy, secret ballot voting. Much like Fairness Committees, secret ballot voting was designed to give employees a greater say in managing workplace issues that have an impact on the entire division.

And more recently, in North America, we created a new employee position known as the Employee Advocate. The Advocate's job is to ensure that employee issues and concerns are resolved quickly and in accordance with Magna's Fair Enterprise principles and operating philosophy. Only employees, via a secret ballot vote, can dismiss an Advocate.

I fundamentally believe that if employees know they are treated fairly and that their contributions are fairly rewarded, they will become more involved in searching for ways to improve productivity and quality. I also believe that employees know better than anyone else what works best in their own workplace. When I was a manager during Magna's early days, I always used to sit down with employees and ask them for ideas on how to make things better. I made sure they had a say in how we ran the factory.

That's why we've always tried to create a workplace environment at Magna where employees are not afraid to speak freely or to voice their concerns. When employees feel that someone is standing behind them with a whip, when they're afraid to speak their mind, there's no way you'll be able to motivate or inspire them. I would always tell our managers, if an employee criticizes you, and you hit the employee over the head with a two-by-four, figuratively speaking, no one will ever speak up again. Once that happens, you've lost your partners in profitability, and you're probably on the road to losing your profitability as well.

It's hard to always be fair, because we live in a world that is imperfect, and people can sometimes act irresponsibly. And I'm the first to admit that we're not perfect. But through the Charter and other employee programs, I believe we created a system that strives to uphold fairness.

When you boil it right down, it's pretty simple: if employees aren't happy, their hearts are not in their work, and they will only do what they have to do to keep their jobs. But if you've got a healthy and happy work environment—if employees feel that they're part of something special, with a tangible stake in the outcome, and managers who recognize and reward individual contributions—they'll become more involved in searching for ways to improve productivity and quality.

It's not easy being a manager because the customer is always breathing down your neck. Management also has an obligation to look after our shareholders, who count on us to give them a decent return on their investment. But we're constantly hammering away at our managers to remember that our first obligation is to our employees. Shareholders come and go, but workers are always going to be there.

BE THE BEST

Pursue what makes you happy, because you can't be good at anything if your heart's not in it. But if you enjoy doing something, chances are you'll do it well. And if you give an extra effort, chances are you could be among the very best at what you do. Money and success are simply by-products of doing something you enjoy and doing it exceedingly well.

CHAPTER 9

REVOLUTIONIZING THE CAR INDUSTRY

I could be the cousin of Henry Ford and he couldn't help me land a contract if the price and quality weren't right.

After a few rocky years at the start of the decade, the automotive industry began to boom during the 1980s. We bundled together the aerospace and defence divisions and spun them out as a separate business, focusing instead on the more lucrative automotive business. It marked the end of the old Magna Electronics era.

By 1985, Magna's sales started to soar. Revenues had increased by 40 percent over the previous year, even though North American vehicle production had risen by less than 5 percent. By 1986, Magna punched through the $1 billion mark in sales—a milestone event for the small tool shop that had posted first-year sales of $50,000 some thirty years earlier.

It was around this time that I became one of the highest paid executives in the country because of Magna's unique profit-sharing formula embedded in our Corporate Constitution.

Profits were climbing, and the more profits Magna made, the more money I made—along with all of our managers, employees and shareholders.

One day I gave a talk in Detroit to a bunch of VP-level executives at General Motors, and I said that Magna was growing so fast that one day we would buy GM. It drew a lot of laughter but I don't think anyone realized I was only half-joking. Of course, we never did buy GM but we almost bought a big piece of the carmaker back in 2009, when we hammered out a deal with GM to purchase Adam Opel AG, their European carmaking operation. Political meddling ended up muddying the waters, and the deal fell apart.

Many of the product lines that Magna still makes today were first engineered and manufactured during the roaring 1980s. Magna introduced a number of new products during the decade—everything from sunroofs to instrument clusters. By the end of the decade, our transmissions and engine systems group had become one of the largest manufacturers in North America for parts underneath the hood.

But where Magna really left its mark, where we truly transformed the industry, was our strategy of creating larger and more complex vehicle systems and modules. It was the better product for a better price formula on an even bigger scale. While most auto suppliers where content to make the simple components that Detroit jobbed out, we pushed the idea of bundling a bunch of different parts into a larger vehicle system—for example, combining all of the wires and latches and locks that make up the electro-mechanical cartilage of a car door and packaging it together into a single door module.

By doing so, we were able to save the car manufacturers time and money when it came to assembling their vehicles. Instead of stringing cables and attaching wires to the metal shell of the inner door, we would give them a pre-assembled cassette with all of the hardware and wiring attached, a bigger chunk that an assembly line worker could simply bolt into the door. It saved time, money, space—you name it. The automakers clamoured for more. If we could do the innards of a door, maybe we could do the complete interior of the car—the dashboard, the seats, everything. And indeed we could.

It was the next big step up in our evolution from a parts maker to a sophisticated modular systems supplier. More importantly, it helped make the company hundreds of millions of dollars in new sales as we began building bigger and bigger pieces of the car. We started winning contracts for modular doors. And because we made interior plastic panels and metal door panels as well as latches, we could stuff more Magna content into the module, boosting our sales even higher.

We began setting our sights on the major overseas markets of Europe and Japan. We established our first European manufacturing facility in Germany in 1984 to produce transmission belt components for the European market—it was the seed of what would later become Magna Europe.

It's funny how things sometimes turn out: more than thirty years after I left the people and place where I was born, my past had suddenly become an important part of my future and the future of Magna. In the late 1980s I returned to Austria to build a new Magna factory in my hometown of Weiz. It was called Magna Auteca and it manufactured power packs—the electrical guts of the side-view mirror. Weiz was a natural location: it had a large, skilled labour pool and was centrally located within the European market. A large number of Magna's managers and toolmakers came from the small towns and cities of Styria, the

Austrian province where Weiz is located. Creating jobs there was for me a way of giving back to the community that had given both me and Magna so much. Many more factories followed in the years ahead.

By this time, Fred Gingl had assumed the role of president and chief operating officer. Like Tony Czapka and Burt Pabst in previous decades, he was one of Magna's greatest builders, a true innovator with a knack for discovering new technologies.

You wouldn't think that the auto industry could learn a thing or two from the way farm tractors were made, but that's exactly how Fred Gingl discovered a new method for making seats. Fred was flipping through a German magazine one day in 1984 when he read about a new technology for making tractor seats. Fred called the inventor, Georg Grammer, and flew to Hamburg, West Germany, the next day to meet him. That meeting in 1984 led to a joint venture with Grammer Seating Systems, and a few years later, Integram—Magna's new seat division—introduced a patented foam technology known as foam-in-place seating, a revolutionary advance that eliminated the traditional cut-and-sew production methods for manufacturing seats. After developing some prototype seats, Integram won Magna's first major contract to supply complete seating systems. As luck would have it, the seats debuted on the Chrysler minivan, which would go on to become one of the best-selling vehicles in automotive history. Our breakthrough foam-in-place seating also became an important new product line and helped start Magna down the road to becoming one of the industry's leading suppliers of seating systems.

A few years later, when Fred was taking his young son for a ride one day, he hit on a new idea after struggling with buckling his son into the car: the built-in child safety seat. It was an industry first—and Magna jointly developed the innovative product with Chrysler using the same foam-in-place technology that produced seats for the Chrysler minivan. Some ten years later, Magna had sold more than 1 million units worldwide. That same year, our unique built-in child safety seat was inducted into the Smithsonian Institution in Washington, D.C., as one of the great innovations of the 1980s.

Perhaps the single biggest technological advance for Magna during the 1980s was the development of the capability to produce large exterior stamped components such as hoods, trunks and fenders. Up until that point, Magna had supplied mostly smaller stamped parts. But an opportunity to move into larger metal stampings arose after Renault bought American Motors Corporation (AMC). Renault had a new AMC vehicle scheduled to go into production but didn't have enough money to open a new, large stamping facility. So we convinced Renault to award us the stamping contract, even though we had never supplied large metal stampings and had no presses capable of producing the parts. The only thing we did have was a take-it-to-the-bank reputation for doing what we said we'd do. Every new product or technology we tackled succeeded. We didn't know what we were getting into, but we knew we would somehow find a way to make it work.

In 1985, we won a massive contract to manufacture the entire outer body sheet metal for a new vehicle to be introduced in 1988, the ill-fated Eagle Premier. When Chrysler bought the struggling American Motors from Renault, they inherited the Magna contract. Magna, meanwhile, built our Karmax division just west of Toronto, a state-of-the-art facility equipped to produce virtually any size or type of large stamping. Karmax began full production in 1987, making both interior and exterior sheet metal body parts for the Eagle Premier. The Premier was to have been AMC's flagship new entry in the full-size sedan category. Code-named the X-58, the Premier was long and sleek, with the latest in electronic gadgets and a futuristic dash-mounted gear selector. It ended up being the Edsel of its day.

It didn't matter that the Premier was a flop: it was our first foray into the business of producing large metal pieces, and it became a key building block in Magna's long-term strategy of providing total vehicle capability to our customers. More than twenty years later, the Karmax facility we built back in the 1980s still remains one of the world's biggest and best sheet metal stamping facilities.

But it was also during this time that the Magna culture faced one of its first challenges—and it came from the man who had helped me build Magna, my friend Tony Czapka.

Tony had a very strong bond with his son, Peter, who was a toolmaker like his father and had also obtained a business degree at one of the top schools in the country. One day Tony approached me and said he wanted me to sell him one of the Magna factories, a factory that he and his son could own and operate together.

But I couldn't do it. Shareholders wouldn't have been too pleased that I let a good factory go to what would have become, in effect, a competitor. It would have set a bad precedent. Next thing I know, other managers might be coming up to me and saying, "Hey, Frank, can I buy this factory?" Tony and I had a major disagreement and went a long spell without talking to one another. It pained me because he was my best friend. As long as I had known him, he was always there for me when I needed him. If there was a job we had to get out, who showed up on a Sunday night? Always Tony. So I kept mulling over possible solutions. I didn't want to lose my friend, but at the same time I couldn't sabotage the Magna culture I had created.

After a long while, I came up with a solution: I suggested a 50/50 split, with the one condition that the factory had to function according to the Magna operating philosophy and the Fair Enterprise principles that every other Magna plant lived by. It meant the Employee's Charter, profit and equity sharing—the whole nine yards. This way, the factory would still be part of the Magna family of companies and still operate under the same principles. What's more, Magna shareholders would benefit as well. I said to Tony: "I think I've finally found a solution that I can justify to the shareholders, to the rest of our managers and to our workers. I think I've hit on an answer that would allow me to stand up in front of our shareholders or the workers in the factory and say, 'This is fair to everyone.'" Tony agreed. The business is still in operation today, and although Tony passed away at a far-too-young age in the early 1990s, his son, Peter, still runs the plant that bears the name of our very first factory: Multimatic.

Following the incident with Tony, I tabled a motion with Magna's board to make it company policy that our most successful operations managers could negotiate joint venture partnerships with Magna. That way, we could retain the very best operators and innovators—the bona fide builders who were making millions for the company. These guys were hawks who had honed their business skills working within Magna's eat-what-you-kill compensation formula. The last thing I wanted was to have one of them become a competitor. Besides, I would sooner have a slice of the profits from dozens of successful partnerships than all of the profits from a wholly owned company run in a traditional, centralized fashion.

As the decade came to a close, we started spreading our footprint throughout Europe. We received our first major customer order from a big European carmaker: a large stamping contract from Volkswagen that led to the construction of new facilities not only in Europe but in Canada and Mexico as well. Close to home, the Big Three still claimed 75 percent of the automotive market share in North America. And although GM, Ford and Chrysler were our main customers, the "foreign domestics," as they were known, began to make their presence felt in North America in the 1980s. Honda led the way, becoming the first Japanese carmaker to assemble vehicles in the U.S. in 1982. A number of other Japanese and European automakers followed.

It was also around this time that we set up shop in the Soviet Union, the crumbling communist state that Ronald Reagan had famously called the "Evil Empire." In 1989, when Mikhail Gorbachev was introducing a number of reforms in the old Soviet Union, Magna became the first manufacturer from North America to open a facility behind the Iron Curtain. We established a joint venture operation in the Ukrainian city of Zaporozhye to build moulds for manufacturing plastic components for the Soviet car industry.

On one of my first visits there, the minister of industry asked me to tour some of the Soviet automotive factories and assembly plants. We travelled by train, leaving Moscow early in the evening and riding for the better part of a day. The trains were spartan. Several elderly ladies would occasionally come around and bring the passengers black tea and cookies. Outside the train window there were hardly any homes or buildings, just mile after mile of barren landscape. We visited various factories, filled with antiquated equipment and assembly lines that looked like they hadn't changed since the days of Joseph Stalin.

Several days later, having toured the Soviet auto assembly plants, I met with the industry minister in Moscow. We had dinner and more than a few vodkas. The senior apparatchik asked me what I thought of the Soviet auto industry. "Not much," I answered. He was a little taken aback. "What do you mean?" I replied, "The way your industry is structured, you can't make quality cars and you can't even produce enough cars to satisfy the demand of your people." He then asked me why I thought that was so. And I said: "Your problem is you don't have a competitive environment." He wasn't quite sure what I meant, so I put it to him this way: "You know why your country always does so well at the Olympics? It's because you've got lots of competition. When there is no competition, even a fat guy could win the race if he's the only runner on the track."

I then pulled out a pen and started sketching my chart showing the world's three major economic systems. When I drew the pyramid representing free enterprise, with the capitalists at the top of the pyramid and the workers at the bottom, he started to chuckle, all the louder because it was coming from a capitalist like me. I said, "Don't laugh. Your pyramid is upside down, and if you didn't have forced and regulated labour, it would fall over." When I finished by explaining how Fair Enterprise worked, by turning workers into capitalists and by creating a string of small pyramids rather than one large pyramid, he raised his glass of vodka and made a toast to my radical new system for wealth creation and distribution.

It was the late 1980s, and by this time, we were making virtually every single component of the car save the engine, the tires and the windshield. We made so many of the systems and modules under the hood and from bumper to bumper that it was only natural that we would start putting everything together by engineering and prototyping complete vehicles. It was around this time that we unveiled the Torrero, Magna's first concept car, a stunning, high-performance luxury vehicle that took two years to complete. The Torrero's revolutionary design foreshadowed the rise of the SUV, and its styling was so advanced that it still looks futuristic today, more than twenty years later. The Torrero sent a strong message to the automotive world: Magna could not only make any part of the vehicle, it could also design and develop complete vehicles for its customers.

I thought the time was right for me to make a pitch to Roger Smith, the former chairman and CEO of General Motors. I came to Detroit and had lunch with him. My bold proposal: Give Magna the green light to start building cars for GM. I said, "Roger, what business are you in?" He looked at me somewhat strangely and said, "We're in the business of making cars." And then I said, "Your main business is *selling* cars. Let Magna make the cars."

I proceeded to tell him how Magna could make better-quality cars for General Motors at a lower price. At the time, GM was suffering from labour relations strife and nagging quality problems that saw its once dominant market share start to slide. Smith didn't outright dismiss my proposal to start building cars for what was at that time the world's largest automaker. In fact, I think he saw a lot of merit in the possibility of jobbing out vehicle design and assembly to a company like Magna. But he said his corporation's hands were tied: the powerful United Auto Workers (UAW) union would never tolerate the outsourcing of vehicle assembly.

We had gone from making parts to making advanced modular systems. Manufacturing complete cars was our next step. It wasn't to be back then, but by the time the next decade came to a close, we were building cars for our customers by the tens of thousands.

KNOW THE PRICE YOU PAY WHEN STARTING
YOUR OWN BUSINESS
Most individuals who start a business from scratch pay a heavy price and face fairly tough odds of succeeding. That's why the rewards have to be substantial. Owning and operating a business means a lot of early mornings and long hours and late nights. If you want to run your own business, you had better forget about nine-to-five workdays and weekends off. It's a sacrifice that most people are not willing to make. There are many paths to success, but no shortcuts.

CHAPTER 10

JUST CALL ME FRANK

There are no bad employees—only bad managers.

B ack in the 1980s, a magazine rated me one of the ten toughest executives to work for in Canada. I don't know what they based their conclusions on, but I certainly don't see myself as tough or overbearing. I do, however, expect people to put forth their very best effort. And I do have an expectation of quality and excellence, because that is what our customers expect. But I have always sought to achieve those results by motivating people and encouraging them to do the best they can. I try to attract people who want to work with me, who are excited to be part of what we are trying to accomplish.

Besides, when you get a piece of the action—when you share in the profits your company makes, which is the Magna way—you instinctively want to do everything to the best of your abilities. You want to produce work of the highest calibre because you're part of something you take pride in, part of something where you have a tangible sense of ownership. You feel that your contributions make a difference and are financially rewarded.

I've always believed there are no bad employees—only bad managers. I try to seek constructive criticism, to motivate and inspire. I never yell or pound my fist on the desk or fly off the handle. It's simply not in my nature. I've always operated according to the principle that there should be a rationale for everything you do in life and in business, and I always try to communicate to others the reasons for any undertaking I support.

I think I'm a pretty regular guy. I don't wear flashy jewellery or gold watches. If I weren't meeting bankers or auto executives, I'd probably be wearing a pair of jeans and a leather bomber jacket instead of a suit. I also don't think that wealth has changed me. I consider myself the same person who got off a passenger ship in Quebec City more than fifty years ago with a few hundred bucks and a few pairs of pants, T-shirts and windbreaker in a small suitcase. I've never insisted on formal titles or tolerated kowtowing, and I've never joined fancy country clubs or elite institutions. When I meet employees or other individuals, they sometimes call me "Mr. Stronach" or even "Sir." I always say, "Just call me Frank."

Employees know that I'm not some suit with an MBA degree who has never seen the inside of a factory. I've worked on many of the same machines they have, and I've done most of the manufacturing jobs they have performed. So they feel that I can relate to them. I encourage them to talk to me on the same level that they would talk to a co-worker or a friend. Because, in the final analysis, my chief responsibility is to find ways to continuously improve what we do, and to constantly motivate, initiate and inspire.

The experiences I've accumulated in life have made me the

manager I am today. I've been without work and without food. I've been discriminated against and treated unfairly. I've never forgotten those experiences. And so, because of my own personal experiences working at menial jobs and slugging it out on the factory floor, I am perhaps more sensitive to the kind of issues that matter most to employees. It is the fundamental reason why I have focused throughout my career on finding innovative ways to motivate the human capital for greater productivity and ingenuity.

Business schools are constantly teaching new theories about management and leadership—they're a lot like fashion trends, popular one year and then out of style the next. But I believe the real key to being a good manager or leader consists in living by a series of timeless principles.

The most important of these principles is trust. When you're a manager, you have to work hard to win the trust and respect of your employees. And when it comes to trust, there are no shortcuts or detours—once you've lost that trust, you can never get it back. As a manager, whenever I said something, I always tried to live up to my promise—no matter what the additional cost in time or money, no matter how tempting it might have been to take the easy way out. That's how you build up trust.

If somebody tells me, "Frank, I'm a friend of yours," I always say, "That's nice to hear, but you don't have to tell me—prove it." As a manager, you have to prove—day in and day out—that you have a concern for the well-being of your employees.

A business or any organization functions best when everything is transparent. Workers are very smart: if they know management isn't straight up or is hiding something, you will never be able to win their hearts. When I had my first factory, I would sit with the guys at lunch and show them the company's bank book. I would say, "Look—this is what we've made so far." I had always promised myself that when I ran my own business, everything would be upfront and out in the open. That's why at Magna I created an operating philosophy that included open books and open doors.

It's critical that a manager maintain an environment where employees can talk about problems that arise in the workplace. That way, if something isn't right, you can flush it out and deal with it. Some of our best managers at Magna didn't even have offices—just a desk on the factory floor. They were always available to discuss issues that popped up from time to time.

Managers must also know their employees. What are their hopes and aspirations and future plans? What are their concerns? And the only way you can know that is if you're always on the floor with them.

My philosophy has always been that employees don't work for you—they work with you. I remember many times during the early years of my business when we would work late into the night to meet a deadline; I would roll up my sleeves and work on a bench alongside everyone else. There is no better way to lead than by example.

Finally, and perhaps most importantly, managers must not only have strong technical or analytical skills—they must also be great motivators. A manager has to motivate employees to think, and they will only think if their heart is in the business. In the end, it is the companies that are able to win the hearts and the minds of employees that will produce the best products for the best price.

TURN WORKERS INTO CAPITALISTS

Fair Enterprise is designed to generate greater wealth, and then distribute that wealth in a way that is much fairer and more broadly based than any other system. Fair Enterprise recognizes that if you don't create wealth in the first place, there's nothing to distribute. It further recognizes that the people who create wealth should all get a fair share of that wealth. Rather than pit workers against capitalists, Fair Enterprise turns workers into capitalists.

CHAPTER 11

SWIMMING AGAINST THE CURRENT

Governments can't give you anything unless they take it from you first.

A round the time that Magna first became a billion-
dollar company and started expanding into Europe,
I was heavily involved in helping various charities,
hospitals and universities. I also served as a director on the
boards of numerous non-profit organizations and provided
advice to various government committees and blue-ribbon
economic advisory panels.

I was restless, looking for new challenges. I was also frustrated by the direction I saw the country taking. I felt I could
make a contribution. So in the spring of 1988, I resigned as CEO
of Magna International to run for public office. I announced
my intention to become the candidate for the Liberal Party of
Canada in York-Simcoe, the electoral district where I lived. And
if elected, I promised to go to the nation's capital and rattle the
cage of the political elites.

For months prior to the announcement, I had been very outspoken in regard to a proposed free trade agreement between Canada and the United States. I was one of a handful of high-profile businessmen who were speaking out against the agreement. For one, I believed there was no such thing as true free trade: there never was, and there never will be. There will always be exceptions and exemptions and exclusions. When I was a kid, and I played marbles with a much bigger kid, even if I beat him I was smart enough to know that I always had to hand over the marbles. When it comes to trade and tariff disputes and access to markets, the bigger kid is going to get all the marbles every time.

What's more, I believed in fair trade, not free trade. The bottom line is that trade between nations must always relate to jobs. Some of the rhetoric surrounding the free trade debate was based on anti-American feelings. But that was never the case with me. In fact, as a Canadian, if I had to choose any country in the world for a neighbour, it would be the United States. I simply felt that the price Canada was going to pay as a result of the Free Trade Agreement, in terms of lost jobs and lost manufacturing, was too steep. And I felt that Canada was not prepared to step into the ring against the much bigger and tougher Americans.

I've never been one for party labels—I believe a politician's character and principles are far more important. Besides, on many issues, I was more conservative than the Conservatives. But the free trade issue put me squarely in the corner of the Liberals.

I told Bill Davis, a member of Magna's board of directors and the former long-serving premier of Ontario, about my intention to run. Bill was widely considered one of the wisest and shrewdest politicians in the country. Shortly after leaving office, I asked him to join Magna's board, where he served with distinction for many years.

When I informed him that I was going to run, he said, "Frank, you're running for the wrong party; you're running in the wrong district; and you're running on the wrong side of the free trade issue." I replied, "I know it's easier to swim downstream. I know it's easier to flow with the wind. But from time to time you have to look in the mirror and say: 'This is what I stand for.'"

Tony Czapka had always felt I was a bit of a do-gooder. He'd constantly say to me: "Frank, you're not going to change society." When I announced that I was running for office, Tony just shook his head. He said, "Frank, come on, how can you be that stupid? They'll tear you apart. They'll drag you through the mud. Who needs it?"

Tony was right. I needed to run like I needed a hole in the head. But once I make up my mind, there's not much that can convince me to abandon or change my course. I had made my decision—I was going to try to inject some business sense into Parliament, the boardroom of the nation.

I came storming out of the gate. Our campaign slogan was "Let's be frank," and frank I was—sometimes brutally so. I said we needed more politicians who weren't running for office because it was the best paycheque they've ever had, but because they wanted to serve the country and had a lot of experience to offer. One of the lines I always used in my stump speech was that Parliament should have more engineers, farmers, doctors, perhaps a few lawyers and maybe even the odd toolmaker. In the final analysis, I would say, we need some good business people to go in there and straighten things out.

Most people don't trust politicians, so I thought I would be more effective if I simply presented myself as I was: a business-man looking to bring some economic common sense to the nation's capital. And while a lot of the voters found my direct, straight-shooting style of speaking refreshing, a number found me a touch too blunt for public office.

I threw one of the largest political fundraising dinners in Liberal Party history and was enthusiastically welcomed into the fold by Liberal Party Leader John Turner, although the national press insinuated that I had already cut a deal with Turner to be made a cabinet minister if the Liberals won—a claim that was not true. The media began tearing me apart: it was open season. Opposition politicians and columnists were shooting poison arrows from every direction. Sinclair Stevens, a former Conser-vative cabinet minister, was unceremoniously dropped by the party as the candidate in the riding where I was running. In a parting shot just before the election, he called me "Turner's little corporal." It was one of the first of many low blows I would have to absorb in the weeks and months to come.

I sank my teeth into the job. I knocked on doors. I really tried to get a feel for the temperature of the voters. I dove right into the nitty-gritty of the campaign. I even got involved in cre-ating a tongue-and-groove design for the wooden stakes that held my campaign signs. They may not have been the snazziest signs, but they were the best built.

I didn't like asking people for the vote, which is what any would-be politician has to do. It was the one aspect of running that I liked least. Pounding on doors in the darkness of a cold November night, with sleet coming down and voters berating me for this or that, I would occasionally stop and ask myself, *Why am I doing this?* But I soldiered on, usually working very late into the night. I was working longer and harder than I had in many, many years.

Like anything in life, the more you do, the more you try to do, the more you expose yourself to criticism. We had a factory in the town where we lived that became a headline story in the local press because of accusations from residents that it was the source of foul-smelling emissions. My political opponents jumped on the controversy as a way to tar me. My son would come home from school and tell me the other kids were saying, "Your dad's stinking up the town."

I always said I wouldn't have been a quiet backbencher. I would have been very outspoken and called things the way I saw them. They couldn't have put a muzzle on me, but at the same time I would have put forth constructive solutions.

I always tried to take the high road, but there were times when I got dragged into the gutter and ended up brawling. During the all-candidates debates, I usually made reference to the fact that government spending and bureaucracy were growing out of control; instead of new factories being built, what you would increasingly see were new office towers housing bureaucrats for one of the countless government departments from four different levels of government. During one debate, my Conservative opponent, John Cole, an optometrist by profession, interrupted me and said, "Frank, you keep talking about these government offices going up, but I don't see any." "Well," I replied, "You better get a new eye doctor." (Cole, a good and decent man, would many years later work alongside me on the election campaign for my daughter, Belinda, in the same electoral district where I ran.)

On election day, together with hundreds of other Liberal candidates across the country, I came up against a tidal wave of public opinion—one that swept into office candidates who supported the free trade agreement with the United States, spearheaded by Prime Minister Brian Mulroney. It was one of the most lopsided victories in Canadian political history, and it would be a long time before the Conservatives would next govern the country. Five years later, the party splintered along regional and ideological lines and was thrown from office by an angry electorate.

I never would have imagined that it would be my daughter, Belinda, who would play a key role in uniting the two feuding factions of the old Progressive Conservatives, help resurrect the party under a new name, and then go on to run for the leadership of the revitalized party. Looking back now, I wish I had tried to talk her out of running. She took the country by storm, a fresh new voice. People could sense her genuine goodwill and her passion for change. But even though she was a quick learner and a seasoned corporate executive, she was not prepared for the dirty, cutthroat world of politics. I am like any father: despite some misgivings you may have, in the end you want your children to pursue their dreams. I was proud that my daughter was willing to serve her country, proud that the people who lived in the district where she grew up and raised her family elected her as their representative. But it was painful for me as a father to see the verbal assaults and personal threats she endured for standing up for what she thought was best for the country.

On the night of my election loss, I spoke to the campaign workers in the same room where I had announced my candidacy more than half a year earlier. Some of them were crying. I said, "Let it be. The voters have spoken. Life goes on." After the election, Tony Czapka came up to me and said, "You see, Frank? You tried to do some good and they kicked you in the ass."

In hindsight, I would have done some things differently. For one, I would have been more careful about getting drawn into traditional debates and sticking to the party playbook. Instead, I would have focused on what people really wanted to talk about. I would also have been a little less blunt, a little less brusque.

Running for office taught me a great deal. I have a much better understanding of how intricate and interwoven different aspects of society really are, of how complex and sometimes contradictory democracy can be. I took some abuse, to be sure, but the experience gave me a good strong dose of humility, and ultimately it made me a wiser man.

I think I could have made a major contribution. I know I could have provided some vital input into the direction of our country. But it wasn't meant to be.

I've never once regretted running—it was something I had to do. I believe all of us, from time to time, have to look in the mirror and decide what the right thing to do is—even if it means having sometimes to swim against the current.

NEVER SECOND-GUESS

Over the course of my career, once I reached a conclusion, once I analyzed something and weighed the pros and cons, I came to a decision and didn't turn back. Too many people, after they've made a decision, begin to waffle and second-guess. You've got to go through some soul-searching and careful analysis, but once you've made up your mind and made a commitment, move forward and follow through. Otherwise, you can never achieve anything.

CHAPTER 12

MAGNA ON THE BRINK

I've never seen a company go broke if it had money in the bank and no debt.

W ith all my years of business experience, I should have known better. I should have seen it coming. In the lead-up to the election and during the campaign, I took my eyes off the ball, and by the time I realized how bad things were, it was too late: Magna was headed for a financial meltdown.

The day after my election defeat I got up very early and went into the office. I hadn't slept well that night. So many thoughts were going through my head. I was disappointed—no question. I truly believed I could have made a great contribution to the country. I wasn't bitter as much as I was perplexed. Why didn't the voters elect the more experienced candidate? It hurt. But I was still pretty philosophical about it. Sometimes things happen for a reason, even if that reason is not apparent at the time.

As it turns out, Magna needed me a lot more than the Parliament of Canada did.

Magna had just ridden one of the biggest booms in company history—a time of unparalleled growth when we were opening a new factory nearly every month. In 1986 we had hit the $1 billion sales mark and Magna was the golden boy of the auto parts business, developing innovative new products that helped our customers cut costs while boosting sales. By the end of the decade, Magna was producing approximately 5,000 different components at more than 100 factories and had sales of close to $2 billion. They were heady times.

But storm clouds began to appear on the horizon, even before my run for office. To fuel Magna's explosive growth, the company had invested $1.3 billion in new facilities, equipment and technology during a five-year period that began in 1983. And then Black Monday struck: October 19, 1987, when stock markets around the world crashed, shredding billions of dollars of value in publicly traded stocks. As the year wound down, North American vehicle production began declining dramatically. Magna, meanwhile, was caught in the middle of an aggressive capital expenditure program to keep pace with customer requirements for new products. We were borrowing heavily to finance our growth, and the company's bank-fed debt began to swell.

Soon after the election, I started calling in all of our senior executives and asking a lot of questions. It had been about nine months since I had stepped down as CEO. I wanted to get my bearings. But it didn't take long before I started to develop a deep, deep concern. A lot of the factories were young start-ups and hemorrhaging cash. The financial statements didn't lie: we were bleeding everywhere.

So I assembled a small team of loyal lieutenants—people

who were highly skilled in certain areas, people I could count on to help turn things around. We had to cut back, but the last thing I wanted to do was to start swinging an axe. I was going to slice out the fat and excess with surgical precision.

We had undergone enormous growth. And when you grow that quickly, you get a little sloppy. Things start falling through the gaps. In retrospect, our management team was fairly young and I left too much on their plate.

We had become financially undisciplined. We had over 100 factories, and many of our managers were going over budget. They likely thought: *Magna's a big company, so what's a million bucks?* But $1 million times more than 100 factories quickly adds up. And every time I went to a board meeting, our overall budget was up another $100 million, while many of the new orders we had booked had not yet gone into production. Before you knew it, our debt totalled more than $1 billion.

Our debt wasn't the only thing that had ballooned. So too had our overhead. I recall visiting a few of our new group head offices, and I was stunned when I walked into the buildings: sleek marble floors, stylish art hanging on the walls, extravagant stone waterfalls in the lobby and luxurious boardroom tables made of rosewood that cost $200,000, my base salary at the time. They made the Magna head office look Mickey Mouse by comparison.

By this time I had obtained a clearer picture of where we stood: the company looked like a war zone, with fires burning everywhere. As the head of Magna, I gathered together the group presidents and laid down the law, telling them that I was going to direct the traffic until we cleaned up the mess and dug ourselves out of the hole we were in. They immediately began grumbling and digging in their heels. These weren't buttoned-down corporate executives used to toeing the company line.

They were iron-willed entrepreneurs, guys who always called the shots. Prior to the crisis, they had had a long leash and a lot of power—and all of a sudden I took everything away. A lot of them didn't like it and they pushed back.

I wanted one of my best group presidents to come into the head office and ride shotgun with me. I needed him close by so I could send him into the plants to put out the fires that were raging everywhere. But he refused. A former toolmaker, he had risen through the ranks. The last thing he wanted to do was go back to the factory floor and troubleshoot production issues, so he quit.

The factory managers, however, were solidly behind us. They were sick of seeing a pile of their profits get eaten up by the elaborate overhead at the group offices. They were Magna shareholders too—and they wanted the shares to go back up. No one was happier to see us slash the waste and sell off all the fancy trappings.

It wasn't just the bloated overheads that were a problem. We were starting to stray from the principles that had made Magna great, such as our decentralized operating structure that kept the factories close to their customers. In the early days, our customers used to send us a blueprint and we bashed out or moulded the part by the hundreds of thousands, and then shipped them to the assembly plant. But to remain competitive with the Japanese, the Big Three were increasingly shedding a lot of the design and prototyping costs—costs that suppliers had to shoulder if they wanted to keep their business. Our small operating divisions were not individually capable of supporting all these services on their own and, as a result, most of these activities were housed in our group offices. The pressure to become a full-service supplier with design, engineering and

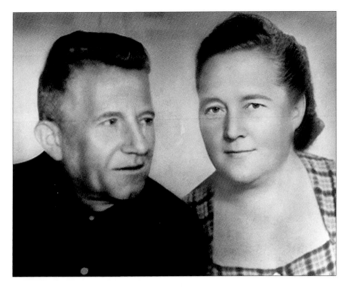

Frank's parents: his father, Anton Adelman, a labour activist;
and his mother, Elisabeth Strohsack, a factory worker.

A school photo of Frank at the age of
eight in Weiz, Austria.

The Elin factory in Weiz, Austria,
where Frank apprenticed as a tool
and die maker.

The soccer team Frank played on as a teenager in Weiz, Austria. Frank is in the middle row, centre.

A talented athlete, Frank played semi-pro soccer in Switzerland before immigrating to Canada.

Frank Stronach shortly after arriving in Canada, in 1954.

Frank Stronach (*left*) and Tony Czapka in front of the original tool and die shop at Dufferin and Dupont Streets, with Frank's used '55 Chevy.

Inside the original tool and die shop started by Frank Stronach in 1957.

Burt Pabst (*left*) and Frank Stronach (*middle*) holding sun visor brackets, the first auto part the company produced.

Frank Stronach (*right*) and Tony Czapka at work in the early days.

Frank kept a desk and drafting board in the corner of the garage.

Frank Stronach (*middle*) and Tony Czapka (*right*) in the Gate-house tool shop.

Dieomatic, one of Frank's earliest factories, located in Richmond Hill, Ontario.

Frank talking to a Magna employee on the factory floor in the late 1980s.

Frank at his desk in 1987—around the time Magna passed the $1 billion mark in annual sales—at the company's head office formerly located in Markham, Ontario.

Frank at a new Magna factory in the early 1990s.

Frank and some of Magna's senior management, including future CEO Don Walker (*to the left of Frank*), were on hand for the ceremony marking the company's listing on the New York Stock Exchange in 1992.

Magna's global head office in Aurora, Ontario, opened in 1997.

Frank visits one of Magna's Ontario factories in
the late 1990s and dons a factory baseball cap
given to him by one of the employees.

Burt Pabst played a key role in
Magna's early years and was
instrumental in helping Magna
break into the automotive market.

Tony Czapka, Frank's first business
partner and a lifelong friend, was one
of Magna's greatest builders.

prototyping capabilities had led to the growth of highly central-ized group offices—the opposite of the decentralized policies that were the hallmark of Magna's early success. Before long, we started looking like the traditional type of centralized corpora-tion that we swore we would never become.

And then it happened. In early 1990, in the middle of one of the worst automotive industry downturns in decades, with our company seriously overextended, with the stock price sliding and sales stagnating, we defaulted on certain debt-to-equity ratios laid down by the banks as a condition of the money they had lent to help finance our growth. Debt had climbed to $1.1 billion by early 1990. Magna's stock, mean-while, tumbled from approximately $37 in 1987 to a low of $2.10 in the second quarter of 1991. We had gone from being a blue-chip investment to something that more closely resem-bled a penny stock.

My main worry was whether or not the banks would pull the trigger and shut us down. With each passing day there were more and more financial vultures circling the company, hop-ing to tear off the best pieces and gobble up Magna. The banks brought in a bankruptcy specialist from one of the big account-ing firms at the time. It was a cold grey March day in 1990, and we were called to an important meeting at offices in downtown Toronto. I didn't know it at the time, but in the looming show-down with the banks, it was high noon.

The bankruptcy specialist fired the first shot: he asked me to hand over my controlling block of shares. In effect, he was demanding that I give up control of Magna. I saw it as a naked power grab, pure and simple. I said, "Who are you talking to? Are you nuts? Are you out of your mind?" I rarely swear, and never in a business meeting, but I did that day. I told them they would basically have to shoot me first in order to wrest away control of my voting bloc of shares. Either that, or drive the company into bankruptcy. I told them that we would all go under before I would give up control of the company.

I wasn't bluffing. Perhaps they underestimated how much the company meant to me. I said, "There's no way you guys are gonna run the place." There wasn't a hope in hell that I would ever hand over control, because if I had done so, you could have kissed Magna goodbye. That would have been the end. I made it quite clear: if the company goes into a holding trust, the whole enterprise will go down the drain. Believe me, I didn't enjoy the brinkmanship. I know some business people do, but not me, it was not my style. Looking back, these many years later, I realize now how close we came to losing it all.

In the end, cooler heads prevailed. The banks did the calculations, and they knew that the probability of us paying back our loans was fairly good. They decided it was better to tough out the restructuring with me still in the saddle. Nevertheless, they dealt with us severely. We paid enormous penalties, in the tens of millions of dollars. The bankers came to our head office and walked through the halls as if they had already taken possession of the title deed. We were at their mercy, and we had to give them weekly updates on our cash flow and debt position.

The truth was, the banks could have called the loans. They could have forced us into bankruptcy. Had we gone under, it would have left a great gash across the belly of the Canadian economy, across the entire North American automotive industry. By that point we had become such a major player in the industry that I'm convinced the Big Three would have stepped in and said, "Hang on—you can't let Magna go under."

As it turned out, our customers were the first to come to our aid. They accelerated their payments to us—they were practically paying us the day we shipped the product, when normally we would have had to wait thirty or sixty days. So we immediately juiced up our cash flow. During the crisis, Magna CEO Fred Gingl was our point man when it came to dealing with our customers. The banks wanted to pin the blame on Fred. They were also worried that he wasn't the right guy to cut, chop, downsize and sell. After all, he had presided over a long stretch of growth when we were building new factories. I told him that the banks were pressuring me to push him out, and he said, "Frank, you do whatever you have to do to turn the company around. If that's what it takes, so be it."

While we were able to get our customers to accelerate payments, we did the reverse with our suppliers—we asked them if we could pay in sixty days or, in many cases, ninety days. Those who refused we stopped doing business with. The head of our Human Resources department met with the account representative from one of our employee benefits and insurance suppliers during that time. We spelled out our situation and said, "Look, can you help us? Can you cut us some slack until we get back on our feet?" The account representative responded by saying they unfortunately had to jack up our rates. My executive took the account rep's business card, tore it into small pieces, and threw the pieces across the boardroom table at him. We were fighting for our lives, and you were either with us or against us.

I had a lot of pride on the line. I'd poured my life's energy into that company for thirty years and I was watching everything go down the drain. I also couldn't face the prospect of seeing thousands of employees lose their jobs. And what bothered me most of all was this: that people would say, "The

Magna culture Stronach created doesn't work." I believed in that culture with every ounce of my being.

When our CFO, Jim McAlpine, resigned, the banks started to get really nervous. They were pushing hard to sell as much as possible. They wanted me to cherry-pick our best divisions and groups and unload them for a fast profit. I said, "Look, if I sell off our best divisions, how are we going to generate profits? We'll be left with the underperforming and old divisions, and there's no way the company will survive." The banks had a single-minded focus on covering their exposure by paying off the loans as quickly as possible. But Magna's shareholders and employees would have been left holding the bag. I had to buy time. So I stalled and dragged my feet. But all the while they were putting intense heat on me: "Frank, when are you going to sell this? What's taking so long?"

I wasn't dealing with my counterpart at the banks, who might have taken a big-picture view. I was dealing with a lot of mid-level executives who were probably thinking, *We've got this big-shot businessman by the balls. He's on his knees now.* And during the meetings, I had to sit there and listen to their criticism and occasional lectures along the lines of: "This isn't your business to run any longer, Frank. This is now our business. You screwed up."

Was there resentment toward me? I certainly felt so. And perhaps in part it was because I was always so vocal, always giving speeches and interviews about my views of how business should operate, how Fair Enterprise could make businesses more productive. I have no doubt some of the WASP establishment guys were glad to see me fall a few pegs. *Look at the smart-ass immigrant now. We'll teach him a thing or two.* In hindsight, I was perhaps too outspoken. I came across as somewhat cocky, a bit of a smart aleck. It wasn't the Canadian way.

But there was no point in getting angry. I had only one objective: to patch up the leaks in the sinking ship and get it headed back in the right direction. And all the while I was comforted by the thought that the bankers would never put us under if we were making money and paying back the loans. But I had to buy some time to get our younger divisions making money.

We had two divisions that were spraying red ink and we moved quickly to shut them down. One was a start-up joint venture that made aluminum wheels, a product line where we did not have prior expertise. We lost more than $20 million in one year alone—it was about a third of our total operating loss. Another was a joint venture with a Japanese company that made plastic bumpers. It was a disaster and was losing about the same amount of money. Between the two joint ventures, they represented most of what we were losing. We basically sold our interest in the Japanese joint venture for a buck just to get it off our balance sheet.

But the situation was never as bad as it looked from the outside. We had highly efficient factories, most of which were state of the art. We had loyal, long-time customers who did not flinch and who stood by us. And we had fiercely committed employees. What's more, the company still had strong cash flow, as well as a lot of prime real estate that we sold to pay down debt. During the 1970s and 1980s, we had scooped up thousands of acres of farmland north of Toronto, in Markham, Richmond Hill and Vaughan—the mushrooming suburban municipalities that border the city. Many of our factories were located in these communities, so we were always hunting for land on which to build future factories. We were sometimes accused by investors and others of land banking—putting company money into non-automotive assets that weren't returning a profit, and we

got a lot of flak for it. But over time, the value of those properties skyrocketed, more than quadrupling our initial investments. So we started selling the properties to pay off the debt,
netting about $250 million cash.

The financial press, meanwhile, made it seem that Magna
was going to fall like a house of cards. There was no question
we were in deep, but the media overdramatized the situation.
The press helped cement the perception that Magna was all
over the map, that we had invested in a bunch of money-losing
businesses outside our core auto parts business, and that this
was the reason for our downfall. But the truth is those non-
automotive assets—everything from a business magazine to a
restaurant—were a minute fraction of what we owned. Nevertheless, the media latched onto them and blew them way out of
proportion.

A number of industry analysts questioned whether Magna
would survive. I worked day and night with a special management team to restructure the company and restore its financial
health. Magna's lead director, Bill Davis, together with fellow
board members Ed Lumley and Don Resnick, were there for
me through the entire crisis as trusted advisors and sounding
boards, particularly when it came to crafting a plan to claw our
way out of debt. They were a rock I could count on. Magna
issued a preliminary debt restructuring plan that mapped out
how we were going to start paying back our bank loans. Then, in
the first quarter of 1991, miraculously, we posted a small profit,
which some Wall Street analysts described as nothing short of
stunning. As part of the debt restructuring plan, we also secured
a bridge loan to help us with our cash flow. The bankers wanted
me to put some skin in the game, so I put up my own home to
help secure the loan.

Then, in the spring, the company succeeded in raising a $100 million convertible bond issue to help pay down debt, and by the end of that year Magna was off life support. I publicly pledged that Magna would refocus on the core principles and operating philosophy that made it successful, and I promised that the company would never again take on excessive debt. It marked the beginning of Magna's remarkable recovery and re-emergence as one of the pre-eminent auto suppliers in the world. Share prices, sales and profits all began to climb to new record levels in the years that followed.

But what I was most proud of is that the turnaround wasn't engineered on the backs of our workers. Over the course of the entire financial crisis, very few factory-floor workers were laid off. On top of that, I made sure that Magna workers who retired during the crisis didn't bear the brunt of our stock's collapse. Employees received Magna stock as part of our profit- and equity-sharing plan, and for many of them, this was the bulk of their retirement savings. When Magna's share price plunged below $3, employees nearing retirement saw the value of their stock holdings evaporate, and it was devastating. It wasn't fair, especially to our older workers. I felt we had an obligation to look after them, since they had been with us for so many years and then, through no fault of their own, they got squeezed by a vicious downturn. So we topped up the value of the shares for all those who retired during the crisis.

By 1992, Magna was back on its feet again financially. Magna's total debt fell to less than $300 million. The company's stock was listed on the New York Stock Exchange, and Magna's share price began to climb back up into the mid-$30 range. It was called one of the greatest turnarounds in Canadian corporate history.

We had walked a very thin line between recovery and ruin. I had come close to losing the entire business. Trying to keep the company afloat while paying down the debt was like swimming with a big cement block tied around our ankles, but we persevered and we succeeded in slashing debt much faster than anyone thought possible. It was a traumatic experience, one I will never forget.

I vowed that Magna would never again take on a large amount of debt or borrow a lot of money from the banks. As long as I remained at the helm, I kept that vow. We ran a very tight ship and gradually built up our cash reserves, which stood at well over $1 billion when I stepped down as chairman in 2011. During the past decade, some shareholders and stock analysts had urged us to expand more aggressively by borrowing money or burning through our cash reserves, but we steadfastly resisted going down that road. I still bore the scar tissue from our brush with bankruptcy in the early 1990s. When the economic meltdown of 2008 sent the auto industry into a tailspin, we were able to weather the storm, while a lot of our highly leveraged competitors went under, pulled down by the crushing weight of debt. I had learned a harsh lesson nearly twenty years earlier—and it saved our company from the financial hurricane that wiped out hundreds of auto parts companies around the world.

AVOID DEBT

If you borrow money, make sure you have the ability to pay it back, so you can start over if your business fails. Once your business is up and running, don't spend more than you bring in, and always sock some money away for a rainy day.

CHAPTER 13

BUILDING A SECOND MAGNA BACK HOME

The well-being of a society depends on the strength of the economic fabric, and businesses are the weavers of that fabric.

The lowly silkworm, domesticated for thousands of years and entirely dependent on humans for its reproduction, is one of nature's most industrious creatures. I saw silkworms up close on my first business trip to Japan, the nation that was quickly but quietly emerging as an automotive powerhouse. It was the late 1970s, and during my travels across the country, I had an opportunity to visit a traditional Japanese silk farm. I was amazed to see the silkworms feeding on mulberry bushes and spinning the spectacular strands of silk used to make fine clothing and other materials.

My guide explained that the operation was going to shut down because it could no longer compete against the synthetic silk producers that were grabbing a larger and larger share of the market. Human ingenuity being what it is, someone had figured out a way to make a product as good or better than Mother Nature's, and at a much lower cost. It was, for me, a vivid lesson in how entire industries can be wiped out overnight by technological advances or sudden changes in the economic landscape. Businesses have to continually adapt to these shifting economic conditions, whether they are changes brought about by technological innovation or changes unleashed by forces such as deregulation and globalization.

So it was for us at Magna. By the early 1990s, I could see the enormous trend toward a global economy beginning to take shape. It was a tsunami that would sweep up every industry in its path, and the auto world was no exception. At the time, Magna was mainly a North American company with only five plants in Europe and annual sales in Europe of just over $100 million. But for me, the writing was on wall: if we wanted to survive the coming tsunami, we had no option but to grow globally and swell our customer base beyond North America.

So in 1993 I announced plans to launch and lead a major expansion in Europe. The massive European market was home to many of the world's leading automakers: companies such as Volkswagen, Mercedes-Benz, BMW, Renault, Fiat and Volvo. My heritage—and the heritage of many of our top managers—was Austrian and German. We knew the language, the customs, the culture. It was our old stomping ground, so it gave us a competitive edge over other North American firms looking to set up shop in this part of the world.

I was spending more than half the year in Europe, initially in Zug, Switzerland, and soon after at Magna's new European headquarters. I planted the Magna corporate flag at a 400-year-old castle in the village of Oberwaltersdorf, on the outskirts of Vienna. It was to be the launching ground, the nerve centre, for our European expansion. Shortly after we opened the head-quarters, we invited the residents of the village to the grounds of the castle for our official opening. They came to hear the live music, to sample the fresh beer and grilled sausages. And they came to see one of their fellow countrymen, a toolmaker from Weiz who had hit it big in the New World and was now coming back home. We came to Europe with the promise of creating jobs and we came preaching the virtues of Fair Enterprise, the success formula that had made Magna one of the biggest names in the North American auto industry.

By the middle of the decade, Magna was expanding throughout Europe. But unlike the previous decade, when we grew by building new factories from the ground up, we expanded in Europe mainly by buying existing suppliers. We hunted for companies that could open the door to new customers, or companies that had unique technologies or made parts we weren't making in North America. Essentially, we set out to replicate the company that existed on the other side of the Atlantic Ocean—but instead of doing it over three decades, we were going to do it in the span of ten short years.

One of Magna's first acquisitions was an airbag and steering wheel supplier in 1994. Airbag technology looked like it might be the next big thing, and we scooped up one of the most advanced suppliers in Europe. We also acquired Zipperle, a European mirror manufacturer, making Magna one of the largest mirror suppliers in the world. We then turned to the U.K. for our next major European acquisition, adding a leading interior systems supplier. And on and on it went, a string of acquisitions at a pace that put us on a path to becoming one of the biggest suppliers in Europe. We would often pick up a struggling company for a bargain-basement price, send in a Magna operations team, and have the factory humming in no time. Of course, at the heart of the revitalization was our Fair Enterprise operating philosophy.

Helping me with the expansion in Europe was a former toolmaker by the name of Siegfried Wolf. Sigi, as everyone called him, became my right-hand man. I first met him in 1994 while visiting a factory we were interested in, late one Friday afternoon. Sigi, who was the plant foreman, left a powerful impression on me. He didn't say a whole lot and I didn't really know much about him, but my gut instinct told me he would be a good person to join our team. Before leaving the factory, I asked him to come see me at my office first thing Monday morning. When I met him, I said, "How much do you make?" After he told me I said: "When can you start with us? I'll pay you double, and with profit sharing, you can make even more." Sigi had a lot of spark and vitality and he was a quick learner. He became the executive in charge of our European operations for many years and rose all the way to the top, becoming co-CEO of Magna.

A turning point in our European expansion was winning the contract to supply the complete body-in-white—all the major metal body stampings—for the Smart car, a stylish micro compact two-seater that was the result of a joint venture between Daimler-Benz and The Swatch Group Ltd.

We were not only starting to manufacture more and more parts in Europe, we were also strengthening our relationships with Europe's major automakers. When BMW decided to open an assembly facility in the U.S., following the same pattern that the Japanese carmakers took the decade before, the high-end German manufacturer turned to Magna to be the main supplier of all the major metal body systems for its new BMW Z3 Roadster, which it built in South Carolina.

Back home in North America, we were introducing a steady

stream of new products and technologies. You name it, we invented and built it: an innovative new way to continuously bend a long strip of coiled steel to create superior door intrusion beams that would help protect car passengers during side-impact crashes; a part that reduced unwanted engine noise and vibration; a patented process to create a single-piece engine part that previously could only be made by welding together different pieces of metal.

Magna was also developing exciting new technologies. We devised a method for manufacturing plastic bumpers with the vehicle colour already blended into the mould mixture, eliminating the need to paint the bumper. We introduced the automotive industry's first power sliding door and then, several years later, the first power liftgate. In the end, all businesses are faced with two choices: either continuously innovate and evolve or get left behind. But at Magna, product innovation was built into our DNA. It was part of our bred-in-the-bone impulse to make a better product for a better price.

Our biggest technological breakthrough of the decade—the one that changed the way vehicles are made—was a steel-shaping technology called hydroforming that we discovered in Europe. In 1994, Magna acquired the technology for a process known as internal high-pressure hydroforming. Simply put, hydroforming used extremely high water pressure to form intricate shapes from steel tubing, basically all of the parts that made up the steel rib-cage and skeleton of the vehicle frame. Although the technology had been around for many years, it had never been applied on a large scale for manufacturing large automotive components.

Hydroforming was a game-changer, a new metal-forming process that took the industry by storm, and made Magna virtually overnight the world's premier metal-forming supplier. Our hydroforming technology consolidated components, reduced weight and improved strength while also providing automakers with major cost reductions. It was classic Magna: a better product at a better price, and it proved to be a combination that was hard to beat.

In 1995, we won a hydroforming contract from General Motors for one of the largest vehicle platforms in North America. It was the single biggest automotive contract ever awarded in North America. The next year, Magna announced plans to build a new, 1-million-square-foot facility to manufacture full-size truck frames for GM. The facility, known as Formet Industries, was located in St. Thomas, Ontario—about halfway along the automotive corridor between Detroit and Toronto.

When Formet began production, Magna's state-of-the-art hydroforming facility was the world's largest fully automated vehicle frame plant. It was the size of twenty-two football fields and contained 450 laser inspection systems and six miles of conveyor systems that transport front module assemblies and full chassis frames. The presses are fed by huge coils of steel, and large chunks of the car—everything from hoods and liftgates to trunks and doors—are welded and sorted by pre-programmed robot arms. By the end of the century, the facility was producing one vehicle frame every eleven seconds and more than 1 million vehicle frames per year. The hydroforming business helped Magna win the prestigious General Motors World Corporation of the Year Award two years in a row.

While I was spending most of my time leading the European expansion, Don Walker was keeping a steady hand on the wheel at Magna's head office. When I first met Don in the late 1980s, he was a young executive with General Motors of Canada who had just played a key role in the launch of one of their new assembly plants. I admired his entrepreneurial zeal and offered him a job at Magna with the promise that he could go far working within the Magna culture. By 1992, he became president of Magna, and then CEO a few years later. As CEO, Don oversaw one of the most dynamic periods of growth in Magna's history—a time when we became a truly global corporation.

More innovations and milestones followed our hydroforming breakthrough. Magna also obtained a groundbreaking "systems integrator" contract to manage the complete interior and exterior systems integration for the new Lincoln Navigator SUV. Magna helped bring the vehicle to market in less than two and a half years, setting a new global automotive industry benchmark for the time it takes to develop a vehicle from start to finish. In other words, we were building cars faster than our customers.

After becoming the first full-service supplier to win a contract to manage the interior and exterior integration of a vehicle, we were awarded another two major interior systems integration contracts with Ford and General Motors, positioning us as the automotive industry's leading systems integrator.

In the meantime, Magna was taking our diverse automotive systems know-how to the next level. We went from building door systems to making complete doors; from manufacturing interior systems such as seats and cockpits to making complete interiors. Helping us get there even faster was our ongoing strategy of cross-fertilizing our European technology with our North American operations.

We capped off the decade and our European expansion by acquiring one of the world's oldest and greatest automotive engineering and assembly companies. Magna purchased Austria-based

Steyr-Daimler-Puch, a company with an automotive manufacturing heritage that stretched back to the late 1800s and one of the deepest pools of engineering know-how in the automotive industry. In fact, the company started by Johann Puch was assembling and selling cars in the region of Austria where I grew up in 1899, four years before the founding of Ford Motor Company. It would become the crown jewel of our European operations, and was one of the largest and most momentous acquisitions ever made by Magna.

The acquisition of Steyr-Daimler-Puch added complete vehicle engineering and assembly expertise to Magna's product portfolio and gave Magna capabilities that no other top-tier supplier in the world had. Steyr-Daimler-Puch not only engineered and assembled vehicles at its massive facility in Graz, Austria, but it also produced a variety of advanced transmission and engine components and systems, including four-wheel-drive systems.

At the time of the acquisition, Steyr-Daimler-Puch was assembling more than 80,000 vehicles per year and had approximately 6,000 employees—the equivalent of Magna's entire European workforce. Sigi Wolf played a major role in helping us land Steyr, and he was instrumental in streamlining the operation to make it more competitive while also injecting the Magna can-do mentality into the workforce.

By the end of the decade we had accomplished what I had set out to do: to build a second economic base in the world's largest market, the market where I was born and learned my toolmaking trade. I've always said of companies: if you're not growing, you're dying. The company I founded was growing bigger and bigger all the time. By 1998, we had close to 50,000 employees around the world, and *Forbes* magazine named us the world's best automotive parts company. Several years later, my daughter, Belinda, became CEO after having served in a variety of executive roles at Magna for nearly two decades. Her great strength was bringing people together and motivating them to pursue a common goal. The other ace up her sleeve was that she knew the Magna culture inside out, having been practically indoctrinated at our kitchen table. They were golden years: during Belinda's tenure as head of Magna's executive management team, the company experienced record sales and profits.

For much of the 1990s and the early part of the next decade, we hit one home run after another. We also had our share of wrong turns and dead ends, to be sure. Some of the companies we had acquired were flops, and some of the product lines we moved into, such as airbags, we later decided to pull out of. When we hit it big with a new technology, like hydroforming, it broke open new markets and brought us new customers. Our genius was not so much in inventing new technologies out of thin air, but in taking existing technologies—often from completely different industries—and transforming them into winning new innovations for the auto industry. Our products were often better, stronger, lighter—and cheaper. It was a combination our customers couldn't resist, and it's the reason why, when the decade came to a close, we counted every single major carmaker in the world as one of our customers.

Most importantly, I had positioned the company for the intense storm of global competition that was coming—a storm that would shake loose and blow away all of the small, weak and regionally based suppliers around the world. Economists, academics and journalists called it globalization. From where we stood, on the front lines of one of the world's most brutally competitive businesses, it was more like global economic warfare.

INVEST IN THE FUTURE

As a business leader, you have to always look down the road—not just five or ten years, but even twenty years and beyond. And that means balancing short-term needs while also investing for the future. If you don't invest in the future, you're doomed to fail. There is simply no way you can continue to compete with obsolete technologies and outdated products, especially in the innovation-driven world of business today. In the end, the successful firm is the one that finds a way to balance short-term needs with long-term business development.

CHAPTER 14

MONEY HAS NO HOMELAND

Jobs are the most precious commodity in the world.

Money has no heart, no soul, no homeland—it will flow along the path of least resistance. That's what I told a room of business owners and executives at a Board of Trade meeting back in the early 1990s, around the time when Magna started to expand globally. It's a phrase I still use to this day, because it's a phrase that for me captures the essence of globalization, the core philosophy behind the relentless force that is reshaping entire countries and economies.

Globalization basically allows corporations to go to low-cost countries and ship products to richer, more developed markets around the world. The plain fact is, there is much less concern for social and environmental issues in most of these low-cost countries than there is in the West, with the result that corporations can manufacture goods there at a much lower cost. But in the long run, if this trend continues, societies in the West will see a decline in living standards.

In the last few years, I have become increasingly alarmed and worried by the rapid deterioration of the manufacturing base here in the West. Wherever I go in Western Europe and North America, I see more and more warehouses and fewer and fewer factories. And you don't have to be a great economist to know why: we are manufacturing and exporting fewer products and instead importing a greater number of goods produced elsewhere—everything from toys and TVs to cell phones and computers. Just walking down the aisles of any major department store provides a startling reminder that very few products are made in the West. Even the fruits and vegetables we eat are increasingly grown in other countries and shipped in. In the final analysis, when a country imports more and more and exports less and less, it will only be a matter of time before the economic fabric begins to unravel and the living standard of its people deteriorates.

To spur the creation of new jobs here in the West—as well as keep the jobs we currently have—our number one priority should be to stimulate greater manufacturing and production in order to generate more exports.

One of the reasons for the decline in manufacturing in North America and Europe is that the current tax system in most countries does not provide financial incentives to invest in a company's home country. On the contrary, Western companies reap greater financial rewards by laying off workers and outsourcing production to foreign countries that have lower social, safety and environmental standards. In essence, we're rewarding companies that exterminate jobs. That must change: businesses that invest all of their net profit in the country they are located in should be exempt from paying any tax whatsoever. If we did that, we would unleash an economic boom on a massive scale.

Make no mistake: we're engaged in economic warfare with countries that have clearly defined and closely coordinated economic strategies. While most countries in the West lack industrial strategies, a growing number of ravenous and aggressive competitors abroad have clearly focused and well-developed plans to make their key businesses or national champions the dominant players in each of the key economic sectors, with the automotive industry being a prime target.

The best example of a country with this sort of strategic approach is China, the world's newest industrial giant. I've always been a big believer that a company should locate a portion of its manufacturing operations in the various markets where its products are sold. But many Western companies are only manufacturing in China so they can ship products back into their home markets in order to make higher profits, and in the process they're eroding the economy of the country where they're headquartered. It's a formula for national economic suicide.

The global economy is spinning faster and faster with each passing year, and countries in the West need to find new and better ways to remain globally competitive. Jobs are the most precious commodity in the world, and in an effort to raise the living standards of their people, countries everywhere will fight tooth and nail to lure those jobs to their shores. But it's the leanest and shrewdest countries, the ones with the lowest overhead and the lowest taxes, that will win the lion's share of new jobs this century.

I believe one surefire solution to reignite economic growth in the West is to reverse the enormous trend toward financial engineering and services, and instead return to our once-proud manufacturing traditions. Our economies grew strong by making the kind of products the rest of the world wanted—products that improved lives and helped generate new wealth. It is only through focusing once again on making things—innovative new products that combine the very best in our knowledge of new materials and technologies with our most advanced engineering and design skills—that we'll be able to create the jobs of the future. I also think we're reaching a tipping point and will soon enter a new era when blue-collar workers—people who can build things, people who can fix things—will make more money than white-collar workers in paper-shuffling office jobs.

I remember when the economic meltdown hit financial markets in late 2008, sending the North American automotive industry into a tailspin that would lead to Chrysler and General Motors filing for bankruptcy. Hundreds of thousands of jobs in the auto industry were incinerated almost overnight. Magna, through absolutely no fault of our own, had to lay off a number of good employees as a result of the economic collapse. It was a sad shame, a real heartbreaker. Many of those workers had been with us for more than thirty years.

Assembly lines all over North America and Europe shut down, and when vehicles aren't rolling off the line, the factories of auto parts suppliers such as Magna grind to a halt as well. Magna sales plunged by nearly 30 percent, a year-over-year drop of more than $6 billion. But it wasn't through any fault on the part of Magna management. The management team was running a tight ship. We had healthy profit margins, strong sales, about a billion dollars cash sitting in the bank—and then the economic tsunami hit. There's an old saying in the auto business: we're the first ones to go into a recession, and the first ones to come out. This time was no different, except we went in hard and we went in headfirst. It was the severest industry downturn

I had ever seen going back to the days when we first started making auto parts for pennies a piece.

I didn't think it was fair that our senior management team took a huge hit in pay when they had managed the company well, so I declined my bonus and asked that it be shared among the other senior executives at Magna. I didn't expect to get a medal or a slap on the back, but the year before, when I made over $10 million in profit sharing, when the auto industry was humming, I got raked over the coals by the financial press. Yet in 2009, when the same Wall Street bankers that triggered the crisis were pulling down bonuses that approached $1 billion, no mention was made in the media of the fact that I rescinded my bonus.

The meltdown was an economic crisis triggered by financial markets in the U.S. that had run wild, with financial institutions operating more like casinos than banks. At our annual meeting of shareholders the following year, I asked, How is it that Wall Street was making more money annually than the combined revenues of both the manufacturing and agricultural industries? Clearly, there was something wrong with the system. When the financial institutions disintegrated, so too did the life savings of many individuals who had placed "bets" on the exotic new financial instruments that Wall Street had devised, hoping these unregulated products would generate higher-than-average returns on their investments. The U.S. financial industry was like a game of musical chairs, and when the music stopped, a number of people were left standing and holding worthless pieces of paper.

I believe one of the triggers of the meltdown was the fact that we have drifted away from a real economy, where we manufacture products, to a financial economy—an economy based on financial engineering, where you have more and more people manipulating financial instruments and shuffling papers. But you can't build houses or machines with paper, and you can't eat paper.

We've become less and less preoccupied with creating real wealth, and more and more engaged in the process of transferring and redistributing the declining wealth that we do generate. We need to be careful that we don't dismantle our farms and factories and end up importing everything from abroad. The implications of this deterioration are critical: a decline in manufacturing capability will lead to a decline in the country's technology base and technical know-how. A strong and vibrant manufacturing sector, with the technology base it rests on, is vital to the Western world's long-term strategic interests.

The manufacturing industry and its supply base jointly develop a vast array of technologies and products—everything from sophisticated electronics to new composite metals and plastics. For example, the touch-screen glass technology on the Apple iPhone was jointly developed by Magna's mirror systems unit, a spinoff product that sprang from our core automotive business. The technologies incubated in the manufacturing sector have applications not only in a wide range of industries but also in the defence industry, which is vital for the safeguarding of our freedom and the protection of democracies around the world. At the end of the day, the continued deterioration of the manufacturing sector in North America and Europe will eventually impact a wide range of other industries, including defence, and it will rob us of one of our chief engines of technological innovation.

If we continue to go down this road, we will lose a lot of good-paying jobs—jobs that will never return. We will experience a decline in exports, and with it our high standard of living; and we will lose a good measure of our economic independence.

To make matters worse, following the economic meltdown, governments around the world have been pumping trillions of dollars into the world economy to keep it afloat. All of this has been done with borrowed money, and governments have shown little or no inclination to curb their spending. This borrowing and subsequent build-up of debt is masking the real economic decline that is taking place all around us. Our fridges are still filled with food, but our high living standards are increasingly propped up with borrowed money.

At Magna, over twenty years ago, I experienced first-hand how destructive debt can be. It's a creeping sickness that is painless and virtually invisible at first. But by the time its cancerous effects are fully felt, it's often too late to recover and regain economic health.

One of the hard truths that history teaches us is that societies come and go. The world never stands still, and societies—no matter how great, how large or how powerful—are all subject to the same unstoppable evolutionary changes. When the economic fabric starts to unravel, every other aspect of society follows.

I worry that unless we correct the problems that led to the last meltdown, and unless we severely curtail the debt-fuelled spending of the past several years, we may face an even greater financial inferno in the near future.

It's as if we're on a Sunday boat ride on the Niagara River, and the boat has coolers filled with beer and wine. Over the loud music coming through the speakers on the boat, we can vaguely hear the thundering falls in the distance, but we don't drop anchor—we keep on partying. And right now, from where I sit, the roar of the waterfall is getting much louder.

USE STOCK OPTIONS TO ATTRACT AND RETAIN EMPLOYEES

It's critical that we don't put in place regulations that might severely stifle the market's creative forces—namely, the innovative managers, entrepreneurs and inventors who are the engines of new wealth creation. For start-up companies as well as larger, more mature companies, stock options and incentives are a critical tool for attracting and retaining the best managers, scientists, engineers and other creative individuals.

CHAPTER 15

WHAT'S WRONG WITH
THE AUTOMOTIVE INDUSTRY?

You've got to motivate employees to not only work hard, but also to think, and they'll only think if their heart is in the business. If you don't win the hearts of employees, there's no way you can be successful.

The economic meltdown that began in the U.S. in 2008 and spread around the world hit the automotive industry harder than perhaps any other sector. The downturn exposed a lot of cracks and rust that had remained hidden when times were good and the car companies were flush with profits. It was an opportunity for us not only to revitalize the ailing automotive industry, but to fundamentally rethink the way we make cars.

So what do we need to change? To begin with, our automotive assembly plants are massive facilities where employees are treated not much differently from the robots that work alongside them. The gigantic car factories of the past century are dinosaurs, and the sooner the industry abandons that model the better off it will be. We need to stop stuffing tens of thousands of employees into large, impersonal assembly facilities that become breeding grounds for discontent. Every employee sees the world from his or her own point of view. But when you have thousands of employees under one roof, with hundreds of rules, it's hard to connect and communicate. The manager and foremen barely know the workers. People become numbers.

We need to develop smaller, leaner, more flexible facilities with no more than 1,000 employees. There is no reason why all of the automotive modules that make up a vehicle—the large, pre-assembled chunks of the car—cannot be produced in smaller feeder factories and then shipped to facilities with fewer people doing the final assembly. These modular pieces of the car—whole transmissions and drivetrains, dashboards and cockpits—should be designed and manufactured to interlock and click together like Lego blocks. The car companies are moving that way, but they need to get there much faster.

Second, we need to create a new model of industrial co-operation between management and labour that will ensure the long-term competitiveness of the industry. It's no secret that one of the chief problems confronting a large part of the automotive industry is the entrenched adversarial and confrontational conditions that exist between labour and business. I believe that most autoworkers would support moves to eliminate the policies and structures that keep management and labour constantly at each other's throats. The ingrained adversarial environment that dominates the industry remains the single greatest impediment to producing quality cars at competitive prices.

Furthermore, the wages of automotive assembly workers must be brought more in line with the average industrial wage index. From the turn of the nineteenth century to the glory years of the 1960s, the American auto industry faced virtually no competition. Carmakers grew fat and inefficient, and unions demanded higher and higher wages. Management gave in to these demands in large part because they could simply pass on the higher costs to consumers. The result is that the average wage for automotive assembly workers just before the meltdown grew to about $70 per hour, including benefits. Today, it is closer to $45 per hour, but that amount is still double the average industrial wage in America of approximately $22 per hour.

What works for Magna—giving employees a cut of the profits—could also work wonders for the automotive industry. I strongly believe that if assembly line wages were more in line with the average industrial wage, but topped up with a hefty share of the annual profits, we would sharpen the competitiveness and productivity of the North American automotive industry like never before.

In 2009, with the aftershocks of the economic meltdown still being felt around the world, Magna came within a whisker of acquiring ownership in General Motors' European car operation. It would have given us an opportunity to apply some of our Fair Enterprise principles on the vehicle assembly line and play a bigger role in the way that cars get made. With GM tottering toward bankruptcy, it looked fairly certain that their European division, Adam Opel AG, would shut its doors after more than a century of making cars. Thirty thousand jobs were on the line. We got pulled to the negotiating table by the head of the auto union, as well as by General Motors and the German government. But Magna had no desire to completely take over Opel. We were only looking for a way to keep one of our large European customers afloat and maybe even grow its market share beyond the borders of the European Union.

I thought that a partnership with a Russian car company was the solution, a potential triple-win situation. Russian consumers have greater purchasing power and a growing appetite for quality cars. And by building Opel vehicles in Russia as well as in Germany, we could have spread the tooling and engineering costs over a higher-volume vehicle platform, driving down the per-piece costs. It would have been good for Opel, good for General Motors, good for the Russian car industry—and naturally, good for Magna. But when GM pocketed billions in bailout money from the U.S. government, they decided to hang onto Opel. GM was our biggest customer, and as long as I've been in business, the customer is always right.

The car industry has now arrived at a crossroads. Unions have to change. And business has to change. In the final analysis, it's about being globally competitive. Magna has developed a new framework for the way business and labour relate to one another—an economic Framework of Fairness based on social economic justice that recognizes and respects the rights of unions and companies while creating an environment that encourages and rewards productivity. It's a small first step—but I believe something along the lines of our Framework of Fairness can be replicated for the benefit of the entire industry.

A number of people thought it was wrong for North American and European governments to provide bailout money to automakers. They argued in favour of letting weakened, debt-strapped car companies go bankrupt, and stepping in later to put the pieces back together. But it would have been too late at that point. The aftershocks throughout the automotive supply chain and the resulting economic damage would have been massive. Millions of jobs in the automotive industry would have been lost forever, and governments would have forfeited hundreds of billions of dollars in future tax revenues. I firmly believe that the consequence of allowing the auto industry to collapse would have shaken the very economic foundation of the U.S. economy. North America wouldn't only have closed down assembly plants—we would have been boarding up shopping malls as well.

But in the end, I believe we did more than simply save automotive jobs from disappearing—we began laying the foundation that might enable the North American and European automotive industries to remain globally competitive in the decades ahead, in spite of the coming intensified competition from Asian countries such as China and India, and in spite of the fact that the industry squandered a once-in-a-century chance to truly restructure and rebuild.

Industry, labour and government leaders need to hammer out a new framework for the twenty-first century—one that will not only save North American auto jobs from disappearing altogether, but also create new jobs and enable the North American car industry to regain its competitive edge. With the right economic environment, the right plan and the right incentives, the North American auto industry can be competitive with the rest of the world.

ENSURE FAIRNESS IN YOUR WORKPLACE

Unfairness is corrosive to employee morale and productivity. If people are treated unfairly or discriminated against, they will become unhappy, and unhappiness is contagious. It's important to maintain an environment where management and employees can discuss and resolve problems.

CHAPTER 16

THE SON OF A LABOUR ACTIVIST

Good businesses do not discriminate.

During the latter part of the Second World War, my father, Anton Adelman, a proud Austrian and lifelong labour leader, was conscripted by the German army and served as an infantryman on the Russian front. A communist at heart, he despised the Nazi regime and sympathized with the Russians. The bleak years of hunger and hardship during the Depression and the war caused many Europeans to turn toward the communists, with their promises of a classless society and fairness for workers. After the fighting ended, my dad told me many war stories—the atrocities he witnessed as well as his scrapes with death and capture on the battlefield.

He toiled in factories most of his life, and he fought on behalf of better working conditions and wages for workers. He was jailed and beaten for his beliefs. I didn't see it so much at the time, as a young boy, but looking back now I believe he was a man of courage and conviction. He fought for human dignity, for the right of people to be treated fairly and with respect. One of the stories my dad told me—one that stuck with him all his life—was about the time he went knocking on doors offering to work for food. A farmer gave him some chores to do, and when my father finished the work he was given, the farmer said to his wife: "Don't put the food on a plate. Put it in the dog bowl."

Shortly before my father passed away, he visited me in Toronto. It was around 1965 and my business was growing. I took my father to some of our factories, showed him blueprints of new plants we were going to build. I think he was proud of what his son had accomplished, and I know my father, if he were alive today, would be proud of the Employee's Charter of Rights and other employee programs I created. He was a communist hardliner, a Marxist through and through, but I think I was able to soften his stance.

I've always said that the original unions provided a great service to society. During the early part of the twentieth century, unions helped to bring about greater safety conditions and greater dignity in the workplace. The old-school union leaders who fought for those rights, who suffered beatings with baseball bats and tire irons, who were imprisoned and sometimes even killed, they were true heroes.

However, I strongly disagree with the philosophies and attitudes of most present-day unions, many of which I believe attempt to create and exploit adversarial conditions between management and employees. The way I see it, most of today's unions are simply political organizations. Their shop-floor leaders are often rough-and-tumble characters, and the ones that shout the loudest, that say the owners and managers are just a bunch of no-good, sons-of-bitches, are the ones that usually get elected.

In their quest to get elected, they make a lot of sweeping promises regarding bread-and-butter issues such as higher wages and guaranteed job security. But the truth is that no union, no company and no government can guarantee jobs. In the final analysis, the best guarantee for job security is to have a fair working relationship between management and labour, one that allows a company to produce quality products at a competitive price.

In the early 1970s, one of our factories in the east end of Toronto was unionized. We had bad management, and there was a lot of favouritism and unfairness inside the factory. Employees got frustrated. When they saw that nothing was being done, they decided to join a union and then shortly after went on strike. We told them: "If you guys want to come back to work then you've got to make up your mind: you're either with Magna or with the union." We eliminated a lot of the problems and cleaned up the mess that management left. When workers decided to return, we made sure that no one was penalized, because I fully sympathized with what they did.

Even if I may disagree with the attitudes and tactics of some unions, I do believe that unions have an important role to fulfill in society—from ensuring that employees get a fair share of the economic pie they help produce to providing assistance to employees who are treated unfairly and need legal representation. But unions shouldn't have a role when it comes to running the business affairs of a company. If a business is floundering, management must be given some leeway to take the actions necessary to turn the business around. In other words, management must have the right to manage: if a business can't call the shots on key operational issues, the owners may as well turn the shop keys over to the union and let it run the company.

From time to time, I'm unfairly accused of wanting to dismantle labour organizations. Nothing could be further from the truth. On the contrary, I want to participate in improving labour organizations and labour relations. I've always recognized the need for employee representation. In fact, over the last fifty years at Magna, we have worked hard to create job security and improve the wages and working conditions of employees. We've put in place programs and principles to protect the rights of workers—everything from sharing profits with employees to creating an Employee's Charter of Rights that provides employees with competitive wages and benefits, a safe and healthful workplace, and fair treatment.

At Magna, we believe these principles will, in the long run, serve our employees much better than the adversarial philosophies and principles of present-day unions. In addition, we are constantly striving to create new programs to provide enhanced job security and increased benefits for our employees around the world.

I could even see that one day unions as we know them will no longer exist. They would be replaced by a national labour council whose mission would be to be ensure fairness in the workplace, both in the way employees are treated and in guaranteeing that they get a fair share of the economic pie.

Instead of shop stewards, I envision something more along the lines of an ombudsman, much like the Employee Advocates we have at Magna—employees elected by their fellow workers who cannot be dismissed by management and can only be replaced by employees via a secret ballot vote. And speaking of voting, I think we'll also see greater employee democracy, with employees even having the authority to dismiss fellow workers who are abusive or lazy. Employees are smart: they know what's right and what's fair. And collectively, through a secret vote, they could weed out workers who are disrupting the workplace, the bad apples who not only impact productivity but who also affect all those around them.

I've never said that it is only labour that must change. The truth is that business must change, labour must change and government must change. We all have to work together—business, labour and government—to remain competitive. And we have to take a long, hard look at how we operate. What we all know is that the old way, the way of entrenched adversarial and confrontational conditions between business and labour, is clearly not the path to prosperity and global competitiveness.

That's why I joined forces with Buzz Hargrove, the tough-as-nails former head of the Canadian Auto Workers (CAW) union, to create a new labour relations model. Over the years, I've always gotten along well with Buzz. We've squared off more than once over everything from union drives and negotiations to strikes. We may not have always agreed, but we always had a great deal of respect for one another. Both of us started out on the factory floor. I respected the fact that Buzz was a straight-shooter, and he probably respected my school-of-hard-knocks upbringing.

One day we had lunch, and I discussed with him the possibility of drafting a new framework for labour/management relations. I said, "Buzz, we gotta change things. If we keep going down the road we're on, if we continue with this confrontational environment, there won't be any jobs left. It shouldn't be that difficult for you to put on one page of paper what's important for workers, and for me to put on another page what business requires in order to be competitive." We agreed that we would try to map something out. When lunch was over and we shook hands, Buzz told me he didn't think the idea would fly, that he'd have a lot of difficulty selling the concept to his members. I said, "Buzz, I sympathize with you: Magna's executive management and factory managers aren't going to be too crazy about it either."

In 2008, just before Buzz retired, we held a press conference at the Magna head office to announce a major breakthrough: a new labour relations agreement called the Framework of Fairness based on social economic justice. Its purpose: to create a prototype for the future of management/labour relations—one that seeks to avoid and defuse the adversarial and confrontational conditions that have often existed in the past and that threaten to hinder the global competitiveness of many businesses in North America and Europe. Its ultimate mandate is to preserve jobs, create new jobs and improve the living standards of employees.

Under the Framework of Fairness, management and the union become partners in ensuring productivity and fairness in the workplace. For example, the framework includes provisions for greater operational flexibility and a clear-cut profit participation plan involving employees and management. It does away with union stewards and even eliminates the two traditional weapons of labour and management—strikes and lockouts—in favour of final-offer arbitration.

The framework is also based on the realization that the best guarantee for job security is management and employees working together to produce quality products at a competitive price. At the same time, in striving for greater efficiency, the agreement ensures there are no compromises or short cuts when it comes to workplace issues such as fairness, dignity and safety.

The Framework of Fairness model is based on the belief that society needs checks and balances. The basic mandate of a business is to make a profit. A business that does not generate a profit is no good to anyone—not to its shareholders and owners, not to its employees and not to society at large. Without profits, a business cannot provide employment, create spinoff work for suppliers and contractors, invest in equipment and buildings, pay taxes or even donate to social and charitable causes—all activities that benefit the economy and society. But the making of profits must be tempered for the benefit of all stakeholders, including society, and I believe this is one area where labour advisory councils could have an important role to play.

When all is said and done, all of the major stakeholders of a business are in the same boat together. Management must constantly think about what it has to do to build a better product for a better price and garner a good return on the money it has invested. Management must also prove to employees, day in and day out, that it cares, and that it is willing to create a safe and fair working environment.

The Framework of Fairness is the start of an evolutionary process. I'm realistic enough to know that the Framework will inevitably require some fine tuning as we proceed under this new arrangement. But at the same time, I believe we found some common ground on a model agreement that will allow our industry to become more efficient and more competitive. One thing is clear: the old labour/management models no longer work.

ELIMINATE MONOPOLIES
Monopolies, whether government-run or privately operated, are a curse on society. Wherever they exist, they lead to poor service, lower quality and higher prices. Competition is the best tool for ensuring that customers get a better quality product at a better price.

CHAPTER 17

AT THE FOREFRONT OF THE ELECTRIC CAR REVOLUTION

Any society that stifles individuals in the pursuit of productivity and excellence is a decaying society.

You don't have to be a great scientist to figure out that the world's gasoline supplies are being drained at a rapid rate. When you stop to think about the amount of gasoline that is consumed around the globe every day, from Los Angeles to Shanghai, from London to Rio de Janeiro, it's the equivalent of a huge river flowing into the ocean—and it's not difficult to see that this river will one day dry up.

Fossil fuels power our vehicles and are still heavily used to feed the engines of our industries, to produce plastics and packaging, and to heat our homes. But the current rates of consumption are simply not sustainable. That's why it's crucial that we as a society put more money into research to come up with alternative fuels and alternative energy strategies.

I believe the automotive industry can lead the way in the alternative energy revolution that will reshape the way we live. In the decade ahead, there will be a large and growing market for electric and alternative energy vehicles. This demand will be driven in part by the rising price of oil and in part by the growing desire of consumers to protect the environment by reducing greenhouse gases. It will require a massive amount of upfront research and development, and the payback may be slow in the early going. And to get this fledgling industry really moving, governments will also have to get into the game and come to the table with some tax incentives to spark business investment.

Magna has always been on the leading edge of innovation and new technologies, so it's not surprising that the company is at the forefront of electric vehicle technology. Magna was by no means a bystander in the development of the electric car. I could see the trend toward electric vehicles several decades ago. In 1984 we entered into a joint venture with a German firm to develop sodium sulphur electric batteries. Two years later, one of our divisions achieved major breakthroughs in the manufacturing processes used to make components required in the sodium sulphur battery, and by 1990, Magna was assembling the first electric-powered van ever certified under North American highway safety legislation. But our customers had no real appetite to produce electric vehicles for the mass market. Gas was cheap, and carmakers were focused on building bigger cars with even bigger combustion engines. Around that time, Magna faced a financial crunch, and the electric-car battery division was one of the first that we closed in a bid to conserve cash.

At Magna, we've pumped millions of dollars over the years

into various electric vehicle technologies. But at the end of the day, we're running a business: you can't have a Mother Teresa approach; we have to make a profit. I've always viewed electric vehicle technology as a win-win—it's both a potentially lucrative business opportunity and an opportunity to do something good for society.

That win-win moment came in January 2009, at the Detroit auto show, when Magna and Ford Motor Company jointly announced a groundbreaking partnership agreement to bring an electric car to the market in 2012. We unveiled an early prototype of the vehicle at the show. A team of Magna engineers developed it in just under six months, an astonishing feat.

I had put the challenge to build an all-electric car to one of our senior product development people, Ted Robertson. Ted was born and raised in Toronto but had worked for most of his career at General Motors in Detroit, where he retired as chief engineer emeritus. He had only been retired for a few weeks when we called him early one morning on the golf course. He hadn't even hit his first ball when his cell phone rang and we asked him if he would be interested in joining Magna, where he could sink his teeth into some juicy product development projects, real blue-sky stuff. Ted couldn't pass up the challenge.

Under my direction, Ted worked around the clock, together with a small team of crack engineers at Magna, to develop what became one of the world's first all-electric vehicles. They built the car out of thin air in 180 days on a shoestring budget—a testament to the drive, determination and ingenuity of Magna's employees. I drove the prototype electric car around the Magna head office campus, reaching speeds of over 100 kilometres per hour, and when I got out of the car, I told the guys we were going to take it down to Detroit and let the executives at Ford take it for a spin. The rest is history.

During the development process, the team designed from scratch thirteen entirely new electrical systems that don't exist on current gas-powered vehicles. We are literally reinventing and reconfiguring the architecture of the car. Around the same time, Magna also unveiled a new electric concept vehicle known as the Mila EV. The futuristic car can be adapted to run on natural gas, fuel cells or hybrid drive and uses solar cells integrated into the glass roof to generate additional power. Last year, Magna E-Car Systems opened a new electric battery assembly facility, with plans to build an even larger one in the near future.

If I hadn't pushed the electric car project with an iron will, it would have never happened. I passionately believed in it, believed that it was vital to the future of Magna. When the electric vehicle revolution eventually takes off, I don't want Magna to get left behind, like some whip-and-buggy maker around the time when the first automobiles started rolling off the assembly line.

Today, Magna E-Car is aggressively pursuing a strategy to produce the world's most efficient energy cell—the beating heart of the electric car. If it's able to achieve this strategy, Magna will be uniquely positioned in the automotive industry as the only company that can build and supply everything from battery cells and battery packs to electric components and complete electric vehicle engineering and assembly. And Magna E-Car is also working on the development of an electric vehicle platform—a chassis on wheels complete with all of the components and systems needed in an electric vehicle. Automotive customers can add the exterior body and skin on top of the chassis as well as all of the interior components and systems that go inside, and then sell the vehicle under their own brand name. If it's successful, and if the electric car industry grows the way it is projected to, I believe Magna E-Car may one day eclipse Magna in both size and sales.

Investment in electric vehicle and battery technology will eventually produce thousands of new jobs and provide enormous long-term benefits to our economy. I'm confident that Magna will play a major role in shaping and building the cars of the future. Imagination will be as critical as the electric technology powering these new vehicles. And because the heart of the vehicle is the electric battery rather than the combustion engine, it opens up the possibility of radically redesigning the car of the future. It's an exciting place to be: engaged in the process of rethinking the vehicle—abandoning the older features of a bygone era, and envisioning what new features will be desired by the drivers of the century ahead.

Imagination not only enables us to visualize what kind of new car we might create, but also opens the door to inventing a completely new form of individual transportation. What if instead of a car—the modern version of the horse-drawn coach—we created individual flying machines instead? I believe we can—and I believe we'll see such devices at some point this century. One thing you can take to the bank: they'll be powered by Magna-made products and technology.

HIRE PEOPLE ON THE BASIS OF THEIR CHARACTER AND ATTITUDE

More than on the content of their résumés, hire people on the basis of their character and attitude. These qualities trump every skill or talent, every educational degree or type of training, every kind of experience. Having a positive outlook is critical. It can spell the difference between success and failure, between overcoming what looks like an insurmountable problem and being overwhelmed by despair and defeat. With the right frame of mind, any problem can be solved.

CHAPTER 18

OVER-TAXED, OVER-REGULATED AND OVER-GOVERNED

If you run a factory, it doesn't matter how productive the people on the factory floor are if there is too much administration up top; the business will simply not be competitive. The same holds true for a country.

About twenty years ago, Magna was seeking approval to build a new head office in Aurora, a small community north of Toronto. The project was going to bring hundreds of millions of dollars in investment into the community and create hundreds of permanent jobs. Job-hungry communities in the U.S. were offering us free land and major tax incentives to locate there. But we wanted to build in Aurora, close to where a lot of our factories were located. We didn't ask for any tax favours and special deals—we didn't even ask that the government approval process be sped up. Incredibly, that process dragged on and on, taking close to three years from start to finish.

In the 1980s, we opened a plant in the town of Nashville, in southern Illinois. I'll never forget the day of our official opening: it seemed like the whole town came out to celebrate. Large banners proclaimed "Welcome Magna" and marching bands greeted us. The mayor was there. The governor came. It was like a national holiday. We never received a reception like that in Canada. In some communities, we had opened dozens of factories and donated millions of dollars to local causes and charities, and we never even got so much as a letter of thanks. I wasn't bitter or angry. I chalked it up to the differences in the two cultures. Still, I was growing frustrated with the bureaucratic delays here at home. At one point I told a reporter that when a new business comes to town in the U.S., they roll out the red carpet; in Canada, they roll out the red tape.

In today's relentless global competition, it's not just businesses that need to become more efficient—so do governments. Throughout the Western world, we have far too much government bureaucracy and overhead, and we're paying for that overhead through very high rates of taxation. That makes us increasingly uncompetitive on a global scale at a time when economies are engaged in global economic warfare.

I've often said that if you run a factory, it doesn't matter how productive the people on the factory floor are if there is too much administration up top; the business will simply not be competitive. The same holds true for a country.

The truth is, whether it's North America or Europe, we're overtaxed, over-regulated and over-governed. Countries throughout the West need to take a long, hard look at all of the hidden costs of doing business that are choking productivity. And they also need to think about what they can do to reduce the inevitable build-up of bureaucracy.

The harder bureaucrats work, the more bureaucrats they create. It's almost like a law of nature: the more we keep feeding the gorilla of government bureaucracy, the bigger the gorilla gets. But at the same time, I don't think government bureaucrats should be made the scapegoat for our problems. It's not the fault of civil servants that bureaucracies have gotten bloated. All of us, to a certain extent, are to blame because we as a society have repeatedly turned to government as the chief source to solve all of our social and economic problems and fulfill all of our needs.

Let's face it: there's a lot of government fat that can be cut out and a lot of waste that can be stopped by turning off the taps of taxpayer funding. I see no reason why we couldn't immediately institute a program of targeted cuts in government spending. The reduction could be done without taking a chainsaw to government programs, without jeopardizing safety, the environment, education or health, by simply reducing government spending by 5 to 10 percent per year over a period of five years. Government employees affected by streamlining government services would receive a fair settlement. The result would be dramatic: after five years, taxes could be as much as 50 percent lower than what they are now, and investment money would start flowing in.

One area of government that has grown grossly inefficient is the welfare system. The social safety net that Western democracies created following the economic turbulence of the Great Depression and World War II was designed to protect citizens from economic hardship and cushion individuals who fell through the cracks. Over time that safety net has grown wider and has become padded with more and bigger benefits.

Decades of government coddling has created a growing class of people who are not able to be productive citizens. We've gone astray from the core principle that government should only set the ground rules and provide a minimum number of services, and embraced a philosophy that government should do everything, regardless of whether or not individuals can look after themselves. And along the way, we've forgotten that governments can't give you anything unless they take it from you in the first place, wasting a good portion of the money in the process.

The key question with regard to social assistance is this: Can we reduce poverty while preserving the dignity of people on welfare and also cut government expenditures at the same time? I think we can.

I would propose that everyone requiring social assistance receive a government-issued credit card with a monthly maximum dollar amount along with minimum allocations for food, accommodation and clothing. The card would guarantee that recipients could buy all of their basic food needs, with minimum dollar amounts based on food requirements for individuals or families. The card could not be used to purchase non-essential items such as alcohol or lottery tickets. In essence, the card would ensure that people received nutritious food, affordable shelter, clothing and other necessities of life.

At the same time, we should also take a closer look at whether or not the state needs to become more involved in interventions on behalf of children who are living in homes where there is physical, emotional and mental abuse, neglect, malnourishment and improper care. In an ideal society, all children would be raised by loving and caring parents. But the reality is that many are being raised in dysfunctional environments, with a parent or parents who are barely capable of looking after themselves due to drug and alcohol abuse or mental illness. Children who grow up in this kind of environment are often doomed to live the same sort of self-destructive life as their parents, dependent on government handouts for their entire lives. We should consider whether these abused and abandoned children ought to be raised in government-supported child care homes, where they would have access to proper learning, nutrition and physical education.

Poverty is a cancer within society and we must do everything we can to eradicate it. Like cancer, poverty grows and spreads if left unchecked. We've tried the current system of welfare for three generations now—and it clearly is not helping a large number of the people that it was meant to help. On the contrary, we've created a system that breeds poverty from one generation to the next. Sometimes, you have to get very sick before you can begin to get healthy again. Perhaps our society is reaching that point now. Perhaps we'll soon come to the conclusion that we've done ourselves no favours by being too soft and too lax, by herding and spoon-feeding a larger and larger portion of society.

Introducing a social assistance credit card will help make welfare what it was originally intended to be—a hand up for those who have fallen on hard times and need temporary relief, and financial security for those who, as a result of accident or illness, are unable to support themselves. Ultimately, we need to create government systems that harness the deep-seated human instinct to do better, rather than support dead-end traps that keep many people living well below their potential.

I've always maintained when it comes to business that there is no such thing as bad workers, only bad managers. The same principle holds true for governments and their citizens. When countries sink deeper and deeper into debt, it's usually the fault of poorly managed governments and reckless politicians looking for quick fixes and easy solutions. In other words, politicians often end up placing short-term political gains ahead of the long-term economic well-being of the nation.

That's been the case for most countries in Europe and North America, where for decades now governments have been spending more than they've been taking in, racking up massive national debts in the process. Every household knows that it can't spend more than it earns, otherwise the family will end up in the poorhouse. Every farmer knows that he can't spend more than he earns, otherwise he'll eventually lose his farm. And every business person knows that if your business spends more money than it brings in, the company will eventually go bankrupt. Most politicians know that spending is out of control, but they're afraid to do anything that might loosen their grip on power. Basically, they're avoiding the day of reckoning that will surely come.

I believe citizens from debt-burdened countries in Europe and North America need to push for changes that will tie the hands of free-spending politicians so that governments cannot spend more than they bring in through taxes and other fees. At the same time, governments need to begin creating realistic debt repayment programs that have real teeth and specific targets. Simply balancing the budget is not enough; governments need to also build in budget surpluses so they can begin to aggressively pay down debt through annual payments amounting to approximately 2 to 5 percent of the total debt owing.

There is no escaping the consequences of debt: one way or another, we will all have to pay for it. In the final analysis, we're destroying our children's and grandchildren's futures. It's high time that we faced up to our debt obligations and forced our political leaders to stop spending more than they take in.

But when it comes to the health of our economy, the measure that has the single greatest bearing is the tax system. More than any other economic lever, the tax system determines whether the economy grows, shrinks or stagnates.

Over the years, when I spoke at Chamber of Commerce dinners or business school lectures, I often used to say that we need to create a tax system that a high school student could understand—something simple, straightforward and clear-cut, with no loopholes. It was a commonsense statement that always sparked loud applause from the audience.

I still strongly believe that. We need a tax system that is transparent, simpler and more geared toward the creation of wealth. If we developed such a system, we could dramatically reduce government overhead and free businesses from the time spent complying with tax filings and preparing for tax audits— time that ultimately increases the final cost of the product or service provided by the business.

The tax codes have become more and more complicated and cumbersome with each passing year, requiring a growing army of lawyers and tax specialists and financial experts to navigate their way through a maze of rules and regulations.

I can't count the number of times during the course of my career when we were faced with a business tax matter that needed a clear-cut answer. The tax people inside the company sometimes weren't quite sure which road to take, so we would consult an expert from one of the big downtown tax law firms, who would say, "Well, Frank, we're not quite sure. Maybe we should talk to another expert." And that expert would say the same thing. After countless meetings, and thousands of dollars in fees, no one could put forward a definitive answer. But it wasn't the fault of the experts, who were merely trying to find their way through the convoluted tax code. The tax system itself was to blame. The plain fact is, the tax system is overly complicated, too vague and too difficult to understand. It has become a drag on economic growth, and a drain on national expenditures, requiring a huge bureaucracy to administer and oversee the tangle of tax legislation.

Why couldn't countries in the Western world create a tax system that was simple, straightforward and clear-cut? The system I would propose is a flat tax, combined with a consumption tax that would be applied to the purchase of all products and services. The flat tax rate would be around 30 percent to start out, but if we streamlined government spending, it could come down to as low as 20 percent, and it would apply to all personal income above $20,000, for example, as well as all corporate and capital income (dividends and interest income).

Corporations that invest their profits in foreign countries would pay the full flat tax rate. However, businesses that invest their profits in the country where they're based would not pay any tax on the amount invested—a reward for creating jobs or investing in technology at home.

In addition, a revamped tax system should recognize that a successful business requires three forces to create wealth: good management, hard-working employees, and investors. All three of these stakeholders have a moral right to share in the financial outcome. Magna has shown for the past half-century that sharing profits with employees is a proven and powerful formula for growth. When workers have a tangible stake in the company's financial success, they are more motivated to produce a better product for a better price. As a result, I believe that businesses that share a minimum 10 percent of their profits with their employees should pay a lower flat tax rate.

Revamping the tax system along these lines—together with reduced government spending—would unleash an economic boom such as we haven't experienced since the end of the Second World War. It would put millions of people back to work. Most importantly, it would create the conditions necessary for enhanced productivity and wealth creation.

Whether it's business or government, the key watchword in today's world is efficiency, efficiency, efficiency. Those businesses and governments that understand this will prosper. Those that do not are doomed to fall behind.

We've travelled too far down the road of state enterprise and government control. We've allowed ourselves to get slowly sucked into a system that stifles individual initiative and smothers the key productive forces of society. And any society that stifles individuals in the pursuit of productivity, ingenuity and creativity is a decaying society.

It often seems to me that we spend more time and energy trying to place a ceiling on the upward mobility of our highest achievers than striving to raise the incomes of those who are at the bottom of the ladder. But the reality of today's global economy is that no nation or state can erect barriers to contain people with great talent or wealth.

The most highly skilled and creative people in the fields of science, art, sports and business—people whose talents are in great demand—are able to live and work anywhere in the world. And we can't blame talented people for moving to countries where they can make more money. The same is true of businesses.

That's why countries in the developed world must create the right tax environment so that our best people and most successful businesses remain here at home. Highly skilled people and investment capital are the backbone of a strong economy. We need to look at creating a tax system that would attract and retain the very best people and investments—in other words, the brains and the money—that will create the new businesses of the future and generate new jobs. If we fail to retain the businesses and individuals that create products and services that can be exported around the world, our living standards will inevitably fall.

With the right tools, the right technologies and the right time frame, even a desert can be made to bloom. A country is no different—we need to provide the incentives and create the environment that will allow our businesses to bloom and prosper.

DEMAND A FLAT TAX WITH NO LOOPHOLES

The tax system, more than any other economic lever, has the greatest bearing on the creation of wealth and jobs. We need a tax system that is simple, straightforward and clear-cut, with no loopholes. If we adopted such a system, we could dramatically reduce government overhead and free businesses from the time spent complying with tax filings and preparing for tax audits— time that ultimately increases the final cost of the product or service provided by the business.

CHAPTER 19

TRAINING THE TOOLMAKERS AND PRODUCT INNOVATORS OF TOMORROW

Innovation doesn't come from executives sitting in an office twiddling their thumbs and dreaming up new products. New product ideas tend to come from the bottom up—from the factory floor, from the blue-collar workers, the people who are closest to our customers.

For someone whose formal schooling ended in the eighth grade, I never imagined that one day a university would name an institute after me.

But then again the Frank Stronach Institute at the Graz University of Technology is no ordinary centre of academic learning. It opened during the early wintry weeks of 2004, not far from the village where I was born, and the gala launch was attended by some of the elite of Austria's political, business and educational circles.

The Institute was established to create a whole new generation of industrial entrepreneurs. With its emphasis on technical skills training and product engineering, the Institute's mandate

173

is to help shape and develop future business leaders who are focused on making innovative products—the foundation of new businesses that will one day employ hundreds and perhaps thousands of people.

My own technical education began one autumn day at the age of 14 when my mother took me by the hand to meet the foreman of the biggest factory in my hometown—the Elin factory in Weiz, with its large smokestack and imposing rows of rectangular windows. It was the factory where she and hundreds of other locals worked making electrical motors and various industrial products. I recall standing with my mother and the other workers in the chill morning air, waiting for the large gates to open to signal the start of the morning shift. My mother, an iron-willed and pragmatic lady, asked the foreman to teach her teenage son a trade in toolmaking. She figured it was a practical profession that I could one day count on to put a roof over my head and feed my family. There were a few hundred applications and they only took thirty apprentices, and I was one of them. On my first day, before leaving home, my mom said, "Make sure you work hard and listen. Be attentive. I don't want to hear any bad remarks about you."

I was so young that I had to stand on a wooden crate in order to reach the vice-grip on the workbench. Like all young apprentices at the Elin factory, I was given a block of steel, and my first task was to cut off a chunk. It took two people to lift up the slab of steel and clamp it inside the jaws of the vice-grip. To accomplish this task, we were given a hacksaw. It was like something straight out of a prison-escape movie, where you see a guy sawing away at the steel bars. At least that's how I felt—that it was going to take years and years to hack through half a foot of cold, hard steel. If you sawed steadily, you could slice through a half-inch of steel per day. As it turned out, it took about a week and a half to cut a piece off. I was among the first to finish the task. I always try to be the best, and to finish first. The palms of my hands were covered with torn and bloody blisters.

Our next task was to file the chunk of steel into a rough square. It was a gruelling and exacting chore that would consume the better part of three weeks, day in and day out, filing and measuring, then grinding and filing again.

Some of the kids there didn't take the task seriously and got shown the door. There was always another kid waiting outside the gates of the Elin factory who was more than willing to take his place. A supervisor was assigned to watch over us. He was fairly strict—at any given time, he had around thirty young boys under his wing and we were all over the map, bumping into each other, dropping tools, talking excitedly. But under the supervisor's watchful eye, there was never any loafing around or excessive yakking.

Once we had our chunk of steel, approximately six inches long by six inches wide and six inches deep, we had to turn it into a perfectly square block. I filed and filed and filed. It took three long, agonizing months to get the edges absolutely even. You don't put a wet-behind-the-ears, 14-year-old kid on a machine on the floor, so it made sense that they would give me an assignment like that. Once the task was complete, the instructor would check it with a square. He tucked the square up against the corner of the block, and held it up to the light streaming through the big windows in the factory. In order to pass, there could be no daylight between the square and the block. It had to be spot on. I'm not very nostalgic, but I'd like to have that block of steel today, as a keepsake. It would make a fine paperweight.

After that first assignment, the tasks became increasingly more complicated. We had to make a hammer with a wooden handle. Then a marker—a pointed, round chisel for measuring where you need to drill holes. Then scissors. Basically, we were making tools that we could use during the remainder of our apprenticeship. And we also learned how to shape metal.

I started each day of my apprenticeship at exactly 6 a.m. It was about a twenty-minute walk to the factory from my home, which sat on the edge of town. After my second year as an apprentice, I had saved up enough money to buy a bike and rode it to the factory every morning. We had lunch at our work-bench most days—and we talked about the usual things boys our age discussed: girls, sports, music and movies—especially movies about America, with its skyscrapers and futuristic technology, and the infectious energy and optimism of its people.

During those first few months of the apprenticeship, we got a feel for the materials we were using, a feel for the tools—their heft in the palms of our hands, and how when we tightened our fingers around the handle they became almost like wood-and-steel extensions of our arms. We were becoming toolmakers, sculptors of steel.

The Austrians enjoyed a well-deserved reputation throughout Europe as good toolmakers, due in large part to the fact that the country is blessed with great deposits of iron ore. Going back to the Middle Ages, Austria always had a lot of blacksmith shops and iron smelters that would melt down the iron ore and turn it into metal products. Over the centuries, the country developed a culture and a tradition of toolmaking. Furthermore, the country developed an education system that emphasized technical skills training and apprenticeship programs so that young people could learn a trade. When you add all that together, it's not surprising that Austria has produced a lot of excellent toolmakers and technicians over the years.

As an apprentice, I was rotated in and out of various departments. In the second year of my apprenticeship, I remember working in the blacksmith department. I was hammering a piece of hot steel, repeatedly pounding away to get it just right, when it dropped from the jaws of my pliers. I didn't want it to hit the cement floor and warp or bend, so I instinctively reached down and grabbed it before it hit the floor. I got badly burned, but put grease on my hand, wrapped it with a few cloths and kept working.

The older workers took me under their wing, and I quickly developed a liking for life at the factory—the rhythms and routines of the workday, the camaraderie of my co-workers and the sense of achievement that came with building quality tools. I joined the factory soccer team in my second year at Elin. I played the centre halfback position, and we travelled around the province and competed against teams from nearby towns. It was a great way to bond with some of the guys I worked with.

One time, I accidentally pushed the drill through my index finger. I lifted up my hand and looked right through the hole in my flesh and bone, then took a deep breath and blew through my pierced finger. I knew that if I reported the accident to the company nurse I wouldn't be able to play in that evening's big soccer game. So I stuck my finger in a bottle of iodine a few times, wrapped a clean rag around it and kept on working. I showed up for the pre-game practice, on schedule, my bloody and bandaged hand throbbing in pain. Looking back, I guess you could say it was a sign of a dogged determination and will-to-win that burned inside me, qualities that would serve me well later in business.

My apprenticeship lasted three and a half years, after which I was a proper and fully licensed tool and die maker. Tool and die making had the highest status of all the trades at Elin, and it was the hardest one to get into. I was now a member of a distinguished fraternity. My mother, who always had wanted me to learn a trade, was very happy. I was proud of what I had accomplished, and excited about the prospect of earning some good money. The toolmakers made the most among all the trades at Elin, and the toolmaking jobs were also the most interesting to me—there was a wide variety.

After I finished my apprenticeship, I stayed with the company for another year. I got a big boost in pay, and no longer had to ask my mom for a few bucks to go see a movie or buy an ice cream. I didn't need much for myself: I kept about a third of my salary, and the rest I gave to my mother.

With each passing day, my hometown of Weiz grew smaller and smaller. I was itching to see more of the world. At the time, I hadn't even been to Vienna, which is a three-hour car ride from Weiz. A lot of Austrians were coming home from work stints in Switzerland, where there was a lot of work and the wages were three or four times higher than what you could fetch in Austria. I applied for a job in Bern, Switzerland, and shortly after applying got word by mail that they would hire me. I packed my bags and prepared to leave. It was 1950. Before heading to the train station, my mother said only this: Work hard, save money and stay out of trouble.

In Bern, I worked at a company named Hasler that manufactured electronic equipment and very fine instruments. When I got there, some of the guys ribbed me and called me a machine fitter, because the work I was used to doing was fairly coarse compared to the very fine, meticulous work they did there. The foreman told me: "Young man, you still have a lot to learn. Your work has to be much more precise."

One of my first jobs at Hasler was making minute components for a high-end precision watch. I had to punch a round circle in a piece of steel—about the size of the sharpened end of a pencil. And within that circle, I had to drill a hole the size of a human hair. It was the kind of finesse work that took my skills to a whole new level.

When I got my first paycheque, I walked up and down the main street of Bern, looking for a swank restaurant. I ordered a veal dish and it came on a silver platter. I started cutting into the meat with my knife when the waitress came over and gracefully told me that I had to take it off the platter and put it on my plate. I was a touch embarrassed, but at the same time I felt that the former barefoot country boy was starting to learn the sophisticated and cultured ways of the city. I started paying attention to the details of manners: how to sit, how to hold your knife, where to place your dinner napkin. I had the waitress to thank for that. When the bill came, I asked her out on a date and she accepted.

I was in Switzerland for about a year and a half, and played soccer for one of the top-notch local teams. It was a carefree life. I was 20 years old, working hard during the day, and visiting the cafés and bars during the evenings.

I eventually moved back to Weiz, lured home by the offer of a job as a tool room foreman, and I worked there for about a year. A foreman's job was a big step up—the pay was a lot higher. But my old hometown seemed so small, so sheltered. Bern, by comparison, was cosmopolitan, an international city with embassies and classy, sophisticated people from around the world—people who had been to South Africa, Australia, the U.S. and Canada. Those were the places where I wanted to go, so those were the countries where I applied for an immigration visa. Canada was looking to bring in skilled tradespeople, including toolmakers, and the Canadian visa application came through first. I'm sometimes pretty hard on Canadian bureaucrats, but I still think they're the best in the world because they were the first to come through with a visa. For that, I am forever grateful.

Nowadays, however, not many toolmakers immigrate to Canada or the United States. In the early years, Magna was able to recruit great technical people who had immigrated from Europe. But when that wave of immigration dried up, and the company began opening up new factories in countries around the world, we realized that we needed to build our own Magna training centres. So when Magna was mushrooming in size back in the mid-1980s, we established our first Technical Training Centre to supply the skilled tradespeople we would require in the years ahead. Unfortunately, we had to close the state-of-the-art facility during the restructuring process in the early 1990s when Magna battled back from a debt-fuelled financial crisis.

Later that decade, once we were back on our feet, we opened the Magna Technical Training Centre, which provides apprenticeship training and hands-on learning for mould makers, tool and die makers and millwrights. Students work on practical assignments and gain further experience while apprenticing at a Magna division. They get a feel for the total chain of activity that goes on within a factory, and they acquire valuable hands-on experience.

Managers with the manufacturing skills and know-how needed to run Magna factories don't just fall from the sky—they have to learn the business from the ground up, the same way I did, and the same way many of our presidents and CEOs did over the years. They were all guys who worked on the shop floor, who came up through the ranks. Our technical training centres, located around the world now, are essentially breeding grounds for future managers.

I had already come to the conclusion several decades earlier that we could not count on the educational systems of Canada and the U.S. to produce the skilled tradespeople we needed. We were on our own. It's a shame, because I believe that our centres of higher learning should focus on providing our young people with the skills and knowledge they will need to develop innovative new products and technologies, the skills needed to produce the sort of entrepreneurs and managers who will build successful businesses.

But I also believe that many of our universities and colleges have become too far removed from the realities of the competitive marketplace and global economy. The world is spinning much too fast for these institutions. By the time a textbook is published, a great deal of its knowledge and theory is already outdated. To make matters worse, you've got a large number of academics doing research that has absolutely no useful application, and there is a shortage of teachers who have real-world, practical experience.

I believe one solution is to establish smaller, more specialized universities as part of a coordinated public/private undertaking. For instance, we could create specialized universities that target learning and research in traditional industries such as manufacturing or agriculture, or newer industries such as biomedicine and space technology. By creating a number of these smaller, technology-based universities, we could generate some of the latest technological innovations, materials, processes and production methods and thereby gain a competitive advantage in a number of industries.

Both businesses and educational institutions should have a vital interest in establishing and participating in universities of the kind that I am suggesting. It's what we did at Magna several years ago when we created the Stronach Centre for Innovation—a centre that involves the collaboration of Magna, the government, eight universities, four colleges and a public/private R & D consortium known as AUTO21. Together, we have developed North America's first combined Innovation, Training and Commercialization initiative—the kind of smaller, more agile, more focused university that we need to succeed in today's global economy. The Centre teaches advanced skills in automotive engineering and production and is currently working on the commercialization of promising new green technologies for the automotive industry as well as electronics and new composite materials.

The objective of the Stronach Centre for Innovation, or SCFI for short, will be to graduate well-rounded business leaders—what we call "Innovation Managers"—who can successfully bring new products and technologies into the global marketplace by turning cutting-edge research and technical knowledge into marketable products. It's a model for how business and academia can come together to create new and applied knowledge for the benefit of society.

SCFI projects include everything from creating carbon-fibre driveshafts to using magnetic pulse energy to bend and form metal parts. We're even working on an advanced technology to turn waste into energy—technology that we'll roll out in our own divisions first and then launch as a new business. The Centre also runs think tanks for our various Magna factories on ways to optimize tooling and material-handling processes or use laser technology for welding and building stronger dies.

Every business talks about the need for innovation—but how does a business actually go about creating new and innovative products? One thing is certain: innovation doesn't come from executives sitting in an office twiddling their thumbs and dreaming up new products. New product ideas tend to come from the bottom up—from the factory floor, from the blue-collar workers, the people who are closest to our customers.

That's why several years ago I created a program called Winning Innovations, or WIN for short, that takes the best ideas submitted by Magna employees and develops them into promising new products and technologies at one of our Centres for Innovation or in one of our R & D facilities, or by collaborating with an external partner. We're tapping the ingenuity of employees to come up with breakthrough products.

We tell employees that we want to help turn their ideas into successful products and services, and in the process we will let them share in the potential profits. Employees with winning product ideas not only have the chance to share in the profits, but also start their own business with Magna as a partner. We're giving employees a once-in-a-lifetime chance to be involved in the commercialization of their innovative ideas, and to get a piece of the action. It's the same formula that made Magna what it is today.

The WIN program has already paid big dividends. In Europe, two employees from the same factory in Germany—car aficionados who go home after work and muck around under the hood—came up with a joint concept that has gone into production for BMW. In North America, employees have come up with ideas that range from recycling waste heat energy to defrost the windshield to air pumps that maintain optimal tire pressure. I'm confident that a number of these ideas will be standard products on new vehicles sold a few years from now.

At Magna, we've got a long and proud track record of industry innovation—everything from developing the automotive industry's first single-belt pulley to the first automatic liftgate. We're branching out into solar panels, wind turbines, golf carts, home appliances—you name it. There's not a product in the world that Magna cannot make—whether it's manufactured from plastic, steel, aluminum or new high-strength, space-age composite materials. We even invented the world's first hand-held automatic skate-sharpening device.

Toolmaking may not be the world's oldest profession, but it's got to be up there. Every product, every appliance, every machine and technological marvel—all were made with a tool, and every tool was made by a toolmaker.

Toolmaking has taken me a long way. It gave me the skills I needed to open my own business, and to turn that business into a global corporation employing more than 100,000 people.

It's been a long journey, one that began on that fall day back in 1946 and started with a task to file a block of metal by hand into a perfect cube. That tedious, time-consuming assignment taught me to take pride in everything I do, no matter how small the job. If you don't possess the pride to do something well, and if that pride isn't deeply engrained in you, then you're doomed to mediocrity in whatever you do, whether it's your career or your business. That first chore, the chore that blistered my hands and tested my determination, also seared into me the qualities I needed to become a good toolmaker. It was a task designed to teach precision, perseverance and perfection, qualities that have helped me throughout my career.

In many ways, I've never stopped filing: I've been filing my whole life.

TIE COMPENSATION TO PERFORMANCE
It used to be that the more jobs you created, the more sales and profits you generated, the more money you made. But in today's business world, it seems that the more people you lay off, the more plants you close and jobs you kill, the more money you make. We've got it backwards: the business leaders or executives we should really reward are the ones who create jobs and produce a profit.

CHAPTER 20

THE QUALITIES OF
A SUCCESSFUL MANAGER

It's up to management to prove to employees day in and day out that the company is a fair operator.

At Magna, we let managers run their own shop. That has always been one of the hallmarks of our entrepreneurial culture. The managers call the shots on a number of production issues and run the factory as if it was their own business. But in return for that autonomy, the manager has to uphold a few basic but very important principles.

The first principle is to keep the workers happy. As chairman of Magna, I constantly preached to our managers about their responsibility to the workers. I told them their job was akin to being the captain of a ship, and as a captain you must look after your passengers. If there is labour unrest within the division, if there is grumbling about unfairness or bad working conditions, then it's a clear sign that the manager isn't on top of things. The workers on the shop floor are the beating heart of your organization. And if they're unhappy, it means the manager doesn't have a feel for the pulse of the workplace; he or she doesn't spend enough time on the factory floor speaking with employees to find out their concerns.

I always used to say to my managers, "Don't get holed up in your office. Get out on the shop floor. Have lunch with the workers. You have to be a leader, not a boss. If you're open and honest with employees, and if you consult with them, they'll walk through fire with you."

The second basic principle is that the manager has to keep Magna's shareholders happy by making a reasonable profit. In essence, it means ensuring that shareholders make a greater return on their investment than if they kept their money sitting in the bank or tied up in government bonds.

Third, the manager has to keep the customer happy by shipping quality products on time. Without satisfied customers, you haven't got anything—you might as well close up the shop.

A few days after opening my own tool and die shop, I landed my first customer. The fellow who gave me the order was an older man, and he was very hesitant to hand over the work. He said, "I don't know if I should give you the job, because if you let me down I'll look awfully silly." He didn't know me at all and I had no track record—I was just starting out. I could see he was uncertain, but he decided to go with his gut and gave me the job. So I said to him, "I won't let you down." To me, that promise was more ironclad than any warranty or contract. This older manager stuck out his neck to help a young guy trying to strike out on his own, and there was no way in the world that I was going to let him down. For me, it wasn't even a question of not getting paid—it was a question of pride, of living up to my commitments. If I took an order,

I always stuck with it. And if I gave my word, I always made good on that promise.

In those early years, I never missed a deadline. Sometimes we came very close, but we somehow always managed to deliver the parts on time. And over time, Magna gained a well-deserved reputation for customer service. We became known in the industry as the company that always got the job done—the company that always came through.

Managing means teaching, leading by example. As the manager, you're the number one human resource guy, the number one finance guy, the number one technician. You've also got to be part psychiatrist, part lawyer. You've got to know marketing, accounting, engineering. It's difficult to find all of those qualities in one person, but they can be learned over time.

Finally, you've got to know the business inside out. You've got to have a firm handle on all aspects of the operation, right down to knowing where the supplies are stored and when the garbage gets picked up. Because when managers start overlooking the smaller details, that's when things begin to fall through the cracks and problems begin to snowball.

A lot of the attributes necessary to succeed in business are simple, commonsense principles such as identifying priorities, acting decisively and living a balanced life. They're the key principles that I've followed throughout my career.

Whenever I meet with business students at universities and colleges, they always ask me what I think is the number one attribute for business success, and I always stress the importance of establishing priorities. Sorting your priorities is critical for the long-term success of both your career and the business you manage. I've been in business meetings where some of the people at the table are all over the map, jumping from one thing to another, with no firm grasp or sense as to what should be the first order of business or their company's key strategic priorities.

Perhaps the most important principle for me is maintaining balance. The demands and pressures of business can be enormous and can take a toll on your personal life. When I was growing our business in the early years, my wife, Elfriede, took care of the household and looked after raising our two children, leaving me free to dedicate a large portion of my time and energy on building Magna. I believe I was a good father, but in hindsight I wish I had spent more time with my kids. That's why it's so important to carve out time to spend with your family and time to recharge through hobbies, sports and other leisure pursuits. For me, it's my passion for horses that provides a counterbalance to my business affairs. But it could be any other type of activity not related to business. It provides you with the opportunity to take a breather so you can tackle business problems with a refreshed mind and a reinvigorated spirit.

To be a good manager, you've also got to have a knack for knowing people and for picking the right person for the job. As a young boy during the Second World War, I was forced to grow up very quickly. I learned to rely on my wits to avoid potentially dangerous situations. And when you live in a constant state of tension like that, you develop a radar. You're always alert, razor-sharp, like an animal that is being hunted. You detect dangers and pick up warning signals immediately. And you acquire a surefire instinct for judging people. Who can be trusted? Who are the good guys? Who's got a chip on their shoulder or harbours ill will? You begin to develop a finely tuned sense for spotting these qualities and attributes in people. But if your life has been all smooth sailing, with no ups and downs, you'll probably never develop the same sharp instincts, the same radar.

The funny thing is, we never want our own children to experience hardship or humiliation or hunger, but in the end those experiences infuse certain traits and attributes that make them stronger, savvier. The things I've seen, the experiences I've endured—you could never learn the lessons those experiences imparted from the pages of a book. You cannot teach shrewdness or toughness—they're the kind of qualities you can only acquire by being in the trenches, by being exposed to harsh and sometimes severe conditions.

When I opened my own business, one of the reasons I was successful very early on is that I had a talent for picking the right people—people who had the right qualities and dispositions needed for performing certain jobs. I believe it's because I had acquired a keen sense for reading people earlier in life, for assessing their character and sizing them up. Of course, I wasn't always right—I sometimes hired the wrong person, or I completely misjudged someone. On occasion, especially early in my career, I ran into a few bad apples that never paid me for the work I did. But I chalked all of it up to experience. In any aspect of life or in any field of human endeavour, you'll always find good people and not-so-good people. But on the whole, I can honestly say that I've had the fortune of working alongside many good and decent people—people who were loyal and true to their word.

To be sure, I've made my share of mistakes over the years. Looking back, I think most of them were due to the fact that I sometimes trust people too much. It's part of my nature, I guess, but I wouldn't change it even if I could. The thing is, you have to trust people and you have to give them the freedom and space to act independently and to succeed on their own. This approach has paid more dividends than disappointments for me. At Magna, I always gave people who worked alongside me a lot of leeway and room to grow. If I had to spoon-feed everyone I hired, I never could have made Magna as large as it is.

I often hired people on the basis of their character as much as or more than on the contents of their résumés. And you can often glimpse a person's true character in the way they treat people they consider to be below them, or the way they treat people who are serving them, like the big shot in a restaurant who tears a strip off a waitress because the meal he ordered wasn't cooked perfectly or took a long time to arrive. When you start out in life at the very bottom, when you wash dishes or sweep floors or clean toilets, you're a lot less likely to act that way toward someone serving you. You look at the people who do those jobs with a greater degree of sympathy, understanding and respect.

When hiring people, the one quality I prize above all others is attitude. I believe that having a positive outlook and attitude is critical. Attitude can spell the difference between success and failure, between overcoming what looks like an insurmountable problem and being overwhelmed by despair and defeat. With the right frame of mind, any problem can be solved. That approach to hiring has served me well over the years—and it's one that I still rely on today.

Attitude—and character—trump every skill or talent, every educational degree or type of training, every kind of experience. Magna was built on the never-say-die, can-do attitude of its people.

MOTIVATE

Great managers are great motivators. A manager has to motivate employees to think, and they will only think if their heart is in the business. In the end, it is the companies that are able to win the hearts and the minds of employees that will produce the best products for the best price.

CHAPTER 21

THE ACHILLES' HEEL OF DEMOCRACY

We as a people don't recognize that government is the management team of a country and the primary motivation of a politician is to be elected or re-elected. The result is that the country ends up being managed via political rather than socio-economic reasons. It's what I call the Achilles' heel of democracy.

Over the years, I've met many politicians from many different countries—everyone from senators and presidents to prime ministers and chancellors.

I've got nothing against politicians—my daughter was one—and although most politicians mean well and want to serve the country, the primary mandate of a politician is to be elected or re-elected. So the dilemma we in Western democracies face is that government must manage the country, but its decisions are driven primarily by political reasoning. It's what I call the Achilles' heel of democracy.

The result is that our countries, to a great extent, are managed by a short-term political decision-making process. What we need to do is find a way to counterbalance the political management of the country with some socio-economic thinking. If we could find a way to do that, we could make government more effective. In business, you're constantly thinking, *Can we make a better product or better service for a better price?* But government should also follow this line of thinking: Can we govern more efficiently? Can we improve living standards and close the growing gap between the wealthy and the workers?

I believe we can, and the government reform I've proposed ever since running for office over two decades ago is the creation of a new Chamber of Citizen Representatives—democratically elected citizens who would provide a healthy counterbalance to the power of political parties.

Here's how it would work:

Under my proposal, Citizen Representatives would represent voters from two existing electoral districts used to elect political representatives. (The two electoral districts would be combined for the purpose of electing Citizen Representatives.) As a result, there would be one Citizen Representative for every two political representatives, or half as many Citizen Representatives as the total number of elected politicians.

Next, a computer would randomly select a list of candidates for the position of Citizen Representative in each of the combined electoral districts, much like the process used to select citizens for jury duty. From that list, twenty or so citizens above the age of 40 who wanted to serve their country and stand for election would allow their names to be put forward as candidates for the Chamber of Citizen Representatives. These candidates would be farmers and hairdressers and store managers and technicians, regular people with practical, real-world experience under their belts. They would issue a one-page résumé profiling their backgrounds and work experience, and the résumés would be circulated to all of the households in the district. Voters would then elect one to serve as their Citizen Representative.

The concept of Citizen Representatives is as old as democracy itself. In ancient Athens, Citizen Representatives were chosen by way of a random draw—the same process we still use today when selecting juries. These citizen "jurors" would take up their role in government as part of their civic duty and would only have to sit in Parliament (or Congress) a total of about fifteen days per year, to vote on major bills. They would not have to give up their regular jobs and would be compensated for the time they spend as Citizen Representatives. And just like with jury duty, employers would be required by law to give the Citizen Representatives time off to serve their country. After having served one full term, the Citizen Representatives would then return to private life.

Although they would not be involved in formulating policy, Citizen Representatives would have a significant say in approving major legislation. Citizen Representatives would vote only on major bills—everything from budgets to health care and taxation—and they would cast their votes at the same time as the elected politicians. The two separate sets of votes would then be added together. A simple majority of votes would be required to pass a bill. However, unlike the political representatives, Citizen Representatives would vote by way of a secret ballot. This would insulate them from any personal inducements or reprisals they might be subjected to if their votes were made public.

The addition of Citizen Representatives would make government much more effective and accountable. The political party with the most elected members would still possess the mandate to form the government and bring forth legislation.

However, for every piece of legislation introduced by the government, the Opposition party would be required to submit an alternative bill on the same issue.

This important requirement—the mandatory tabling of alternative legislation—would enable the Opposition to go beyond the role of critic by offering constructive options to government legislation. In other words, the Opposition would be forced to become part of the solution. This reform would also go a long way toward eliminating the political grandstanding and knee-jerk obstructionism built into our present system.

Removed from the straitjacket of party discipline, removed from the influence of special interests, Citizen Representatives would bring a much more pragmatic approach to managing the affairs of the country. I strongly believe this new political framework would address the structural shortcomings of our present system by blending short-term political imperatives with much-needed longer-term socio-economic considerations. What's more, Citizen Representatives would be much more inclined to place the country's socio-economic welfare and long-term national interests ahead of political considerations or partisan views, since they wouldn't be beholden to any political party or leader. They would have one overriding goal or objective: the best interests of the country.

The great statesman and parliamentarian Winston Churchill at one time advocated a concept similar to the Chamber of Citizen Representatives. Churchill thought that partisan politics and "political brawling" made the party-dominated House of Commons "unsuited" to deal with economic matters of national importance. In plain English, Churchill felt we had too many politicians. He argued for the creation of a non-political body or chamber because he believed that elected politicians would always put their own short-term political interests ahead of the long-term economic interests of the country.

My government reform proposal would certainly go a long way toward eliminating many of the dysfunctional aspects of our current system, where political pork-barrelling takes precedence over economic considerations; where the public will to curtail spending and hold the line on tax increases is ignored; and where taxpayers watch helplessly on the sidelines as governments ram through spending bills and other pieces of legislation that hit people in their pocketbooks and have long-term negative consequences for our economy and standard of living. Our system of government is broken, and everyone can feel it in their bones.

Of this you can be sure: countries that place political wrangling and partisan issues ahead of economic imperatives will suffer lower living standards in the years ahead. But those countries that have an effective management system in place for dealing with national and global issues will prosper. Because the well-being of a nation ultimately depends upon the strength of its economic fabric, we need to ensure that the management decisions of government are also driven by economic considerations.

By modernizing our government management system, we could reinvigorate and redemocratize our political institutions and loosen the bottlenecks that have stymied real economic progress. We would finally break free from the paralysis of party politics.

The Chamber of Citizen Representatives would help depoliticize the running of the country, and it would bring new ideas to the table of government. We would slowly rid ourselves of empty politics and put the running of the country on the straight and narrow.

Who wouldn't vote for that?

PROMOTE LIFESTYLE EDUCATION AND SPORTS CHARACTER

We need to look at the many non-academic aspects of education that help develop well-adjusted citizens who will contribute to the social and economic well-being of society later in life. I call this approach "lifestyle education"—the teaching of basic principles, such as nutrition, that will enable young people to lead healthy, balanced and productive lives. This approach includes instilling a "sports character" in students through a greater focus on sports activities and other athletic endeavours.

CHAPTER 22

SELL YOUR WRISTWATCH AND BUY AN ALARM CLOCK

I believe that individuals everywhere have two basic desires: first, they want to have personal freedom, which in essence means they want the right to choose their own road to happiness; second, they want economic freedom, which means they want to be financially independent.

I get great pleasure talking to students. Their minds are wide open and they're hungry to learn some of the secrets of my success.

Whenever I give a talk to college or university students, I always begin by saying that success in life can only be measured by the degree of happiness you reach. And then I always add: "But let me tell you, in my experience, it's a lot easier to be happy if you have some money." The really eager students ask me what it takes to get to the top, to be the best.

When you're in your early twenties, you don't really know yourself. So you've got to try your hand at many different jobs in order to find your niche. I tell students: Find out what you like to do, and then set out to be the best in your field. Pursue what makes you happy, because you can't be good at anything if your heart's not in it. But if you enjoy doing something, chances are you'll do it well. And if you give an extra effort, chances are you could be among the very best at what you do. When you do something you enjoy and you do it exceedingly well, money and success are simply by-products.

For people thinking about starting their own business, my advice is to do some research and consider your own experiences purchasing various products and services. There's an enormous amount of mediocrity in the marketplace, and we've all felt the frustration of buying a bad product or getting poor service. Zero in on an area where you think you can do something better. The opportunities are endless. But before you start your own business, you've got to work in that field or industry for a few years to learn the nitty-gritty details, all the ins and outs.

If you borrow money, make sure you have the ability to pay it back, so you can start over if the business fails. Once your business is up and running, don't spend more than you bring in, and always sock some money away for a rainy day. I've never yet seen a business with money in the bank that went broke.

I was once on a business panel with some other entrepreneurs discussing the topic of starting your own business. A man in the audience stood up and complained bitterly to the panel about how the banks were unfair and discriminatory, having turned him down for a loan to start a business. A lot of the people in the crowd agreed, saying the banks were to blame for not giving them the start-up capital they needed. So I asked the man who had griped about unfair treatment, "How much of your own money were you going to put up?" And he said,

"None." I replied, "Why would the bank lend you some money if you're not willing to invest in your own business?" As soon as I said that, the room went quiet. I then told the audience of would-be entrepreneurs that starting your own business was a lot of long hours and hard work and cutting back on your living expenses—not the sort of advice they were hoping to hear.

When you have a small company, you've got to do everything. But when you get a little bigger, when you're no longer involved in all of the minute details, that's when business ownership starts to become more enjoyable. At that point, business isn't work anymore—it's more like playing a sport. Creating jobs and giving people the chance to do what they love to do—that was for me one of the richest rewards of running my own business.

But probably the most important bit of advice I give to would-be entrepreneurs and young people striking out on their own is the following: sell your wristwatch and buy an alarm clock. Owning and operating a business means a lot of early mornings and long hours and late nights. If you want to run your own business, you had better forget about nine-to-five workdays and weekends off. It's a sacrifice that most people are not willing to make. There are many paths to success, but no short cuts.

Over the course of my career I sacrificed a great deal and worked very hard, investing a lot of time and money to build a business. But I did this so that I could make the business a success and eventually reap the rewards of that success by attaining economic freedom. That's what drove me.

It's why I strongly believe that society must ensure that there is a reward system for entrepreneurs. If there were no tangible financial rewards associated with starting a business, then no one in their right mind would risk their hard-earned savings and the enormous investment of personal time and effort required to build a business from the ground up. Consider the industry I've worked in most of my life. Why would anyone invest money to build a factory, buy machines and hire employees to manufacture products if they could make more money by buying government bonds? Most individuals who start a business from scratch pay a heavy price and face fairly tough odds of succeeding. That's why the rewards have to be substantial.

One of my main concerns nowadays is that we're creating an economic environment that is no longer conducive to entrepreneurship. We're strangling the market's creative forces—the entrepreneurs and inventors who create wealth. And we're killing the entrepreneurial spirit. Could a young entrepreneur build a company like Magna in today's over-regulated environment? I'm not quite sure he or she could.

I'm always leery of people who say money doesn't matter. The truth is, money can be a great motivator, even if it is only a tool for achieving other ends. And money can never be your only goal: as soon as you become preoccupied with only making money, there's no way you can achieve greatness or excellence.

Our society needs people who go out on a limb to invent and develop new products and services, people who push their physical and mental abilities to the limit in order to advance society and improve living conditions. I have a concern, however, that we're slowly stamping out all the rewards that encourage people to become entrepreneurs and inventors. If we remove the incentives to strike out on your own, then we'll lose a critical element of what drives wealth creation.

When I look back at my own career and add up all the hours I worked, it's incredible, really. There were times when I worked two or three days and nights straight to finish an order. During the early years of my business, I'd occasionally take a brief break while working on a Saturday or Sunday. I would sit under an old chestnut tree outside the factory to get some fresh air and sunshine. I'd see young couples buying some ice cream or going to a movie, and I'd sometimes think: *Why am I doing this?* I was stuck there bashing metal to meet a deadline, wishing I hadn't taken the order, hadn't made that promise to a customer. But when you're in business for yourself, especially when you're younger, you have to sacrifice. You've got to knuckle under and take some lumps along the way.

Running and growing the business is like being on a merry-go-round. You get on and it goes faster and faster, and it sometimes seems that you can't get off. But that's the beauty of being your own boss, of building your own business. There comes a time when you decide to slow down, to get off the merry-go-round and have the freedom to do whatever you want. That's what I did when I cashed out at Magna. I built Magna so that I could one day be economically free, and through the Fair Enterprise success-sharing engine I created, I wanted to give everyone else who worked there a shot at economic freedom as well. If I could do it all over again, I'd do some things a little differently, no question, but I'd do it all over just the same. Although I paid a heavy price, the rewards were immeasurable, and the reward I treasure above all others is my economic freedom. I am free, totally free, and there is no greater feeling in the world than that.

KNOW YOUR EMPLOYEES

Managers must know their employees. And the only way you can know your employees is if you are always on the floor with them. It's also critical that a manager maintain an environment where employees can talk about problems that arise in the workplace. That way, if something isn't right, you can flush it out and deal with it. And a good manager will always encourage employees to come forward with new ideas and constructive criticism.

CHAPTER 23

IF THE TURTLE DIDN'T STICK
ITS NECK OUT . . .

Good managers don't fall from the sky.

D uring the course of my career, I've done a lot of deals with Japanese business people, and Magna has signed a number of strategic partnerships with Japanese companies over the years. When I have lunch with Japanese business leaders, they often say to me, "You know, Frank, we feel sorry for you business executives in Europe and North America. You're always under the gun to boost short-term profits for your shareholders and you have to manage your company on a quarterly basis. It must be pretty hard to set a course for the future." And to a great extent the Japanese are right.

For some shareholders, especially those driven by short-term profit taking, the roller-coaster fluctuations of a stock price during the course of a few hours can feel like a lifetime. Most of the shareholders of large public companies today are mammoth financial institutions and pension funds. And these institutional shareholders are focused mainly on maximizing short-term results and quarterly profits. They don't want to see a company branching out into a new line of business, for example, since that carries a large element of risk and eats into the short-term profits. They also don't want to see a company plowing too much money into product research and development for the same reason—it reduces short-term profitability, even if the R & D initiatives have the potential to return greater profits years later. So the dilemma faced by the managers of large public companies in the West is this: How does the company balance the need to boost profits in the short term while still investing in the future and keeping all of the company's stakeholders pulling in the same direction?

As the founder and former controlling shareholder of Magna, I always looked down the road—not just five or ten years, but even twenty years and beyond. And that means planting some seeds in the ground today if you want to see them come to fruition in ten or twenty years. It's like the walnut business: if you want to be a supplier of walnuts, you've got to wait about twenty-five or thirty years before the trees are full-grown and you're able to start harvesting your product. The same holds true in business, with the exception that you can't ignore short-term productivity and profitability. And from the shareholder's point of view, the short term means the current quarter.

So as a business manager and leader you try to achieve a balance between shareholders' short-term interests and the longer-term interests of the company. A business leader has to think about all of the firm's stakeholders, and ask the following questions: What do we have to do to maintain and create jobs? Which direction is our industry headed? What are the new technologies and products on the horizon? In other words, what research do you have to carry out today to still be in business a decade later, because research is the foundation of the future? At Magna, because I was the controlling shareholder, our executives didn't always have a gun pointed at their heads to produce short-term profits. We could undertake certain business projects or developments knowing that they might not make a profit for a few years. We were also able to sit down and plan for five to ten and even twenty years down the road without the enormous pressure that some firms face. For example, we laid the groundwork for the development of our large automotive systems groups back in the 1980s. When I established Magna's unique Corporate Constitution, I made research and development one of the key pillars, long before product innovation became a business buzzword. The R & D principle of Magna's Constitution requires that the company allocate a minimum of 7 percent of its profit before tax to ensure Magna's long-term viability. Companies that don't invest in the future are doomed to fail. There's simply no way they can continue to compete with obsolete technologies and outdated products, especially in the innovation-driven world of business today. In the end, the successful firm is the one that finds a way to manage both the short-term needs of shareholders and the long-term needs of new business development.

Balance is the most important word in my vocabulary, the state I pursue in my personal life and in business. And balance should be the most important goal of any business manager, whether it's balancing present objectives with future goals, or balancing the needs of different stakeholders. Balance is one of the key features of the Corporate Constitution I created. It attempts to strike a balance between the rights of management, employees and shareholders, the three driving forces of our business. If there is no balance, it's only a matter of time before things begin to break down and the business no longer functions properly.

I think success in business is really a question of common sense. When you boil it right down, business is not that difficult or complicated. It's really all about solving problems. This is well captured in the joke about the business owner who ran a job ad for the position of CEO. The ad read: "Looking for someone to run my business and take all my worries off my hands. Will pay a salary of $5 million per year." The owner interviewed a number of candidates, and then selected the person who would become the new CEO. At the conclusion of the interview, the two men shook hands. The owner said, "Now that I've found someone who will take care of all my worries, I can step down and retire. Before you begin, do you have any questions?" "Yes," said the newly hired CEO. "How do I get paid?" The owner replied, "That's your first worry."

Being decisive is another factor that is critical to success. Over the course of my career, once I reached a conclusion, once I analyzed something and weighed the pros and cons, I came to a decision and didn't turn back. Too many people, after they've made a decision, begin to waffle and second-guess. You've got to go through some soul-searching and careful analysis, but once you've made up your mind and made a commitment, move forward and follow through. Otherwise, you can never achieve anything.

Several years ago we made the strategic decision to move into Russia in a big way. There were a lot of risks attached, but after painstaking research, we determined that Russia was where we could really grow our business. We've been opening more and more factories in Russia, which is on track to surpass Germany as Europe's largest producer of vehicles. I've met President Vladimir Putin on several occasions. He's very sharp, a good listener with a dry sense of humour. He came to one of our official openings a few years back, surrounded by cameras, reporters, aides and security personnel. He spoke to me in fluent German, and asked me to explain to Magna's new Russian employees why we opened a plant in Russia, and what our plans for the future were. He then proceeded to translate every word I said into Russian. I sincerely believe he wants to build a robust middle class in Russia, because the middle class is the backbone of a strong economy and a healthy democracy. But he's got a very difficult job in front of him, and Russia will go through a lot of growing pains.

Naturally, there will be times when you make a wrong turn or go down a dead end, but even then, you can't allow yourself to get bogged down by indecision and second-guessing. You have to pause briefly and look back to learn from the past, but after that you've got to continue striding into the future.

In the end, the most vital undertaking of any manager is measuring risk, and making the call on whether to proceed with a plan or not. It's about having the smarts to calculate risk, and the guts to go forward, knowing all the while that the knives will come out if the plan fails.

Throughout my career, I've had to butt heads with people inside and outside the company who always came up with a thousand good reasons for not doing something. Along the way, I made my share of mistakes. Of course, as I've said, if I could do it all over again, I would do some things differently. But a number of the projects I championed were home runs. They opened up new terrain for the company: lucrative product lines, more customers, bigger markets. Had we not ventured out all those times, we'd probably be a $500-million Canadian company today instead of a $30-billion multinational.

There will always be risks attached to any course of action or direction you take, but I live by the old adage that if the turtle didn't stick its neck out, it would never make any progress.

MAINTAIN BALANCE

The demands and pressures of business can be enormous and can take a toll on your personal life. That's why it's so important to carve out time to spend with your family and time to recharge through hobbies, sports and other leisure pursuits. It gives your mind a rest from the details and pressures of business and provides you with the opportunity to take a breather so you can tackle business problems with a refreshed mind and a reinvigorated spirit.

CHAPTER 24

REWARDING THE WEALTH CREATORS

When you do something well, money is a by-product.

It's a scene that has played out over and over again in the past decade: top executives jumping off a sinking ship into life rafts, and by the time employees and shareholders realize the ship's going under, it's too late—the executives have made off with all the gold, and everyone else goes down with the ship.

Whether it was Enron or a long list of other companies, it was always the same story: senior executives with sizeable stock options bent and twisted the accounting rules, then cashed in their stocks before the rest of the world learned about the firm's financial rot. Who can blame investors for being angry or government regulators for wanting to clamp down on the way publicly traded companies operate?

It's understandable that investors and regulators would want to change the rules to prevent senior managers from cashing out their stock options prior to public disclosure of any financial difficulty or wrongdoing.

But we have to be careful that we don't overreact in terms of regulating the stock market and the granting of stock options, when a simple fix is all that is required.

I'm increasingly worried that we've gone overboard and put in place regulations that will severely stifle the market's creative forces—namely, the innovative managers, entrepreneurs and inventors who are the engines of new wealth creation. For start-up companies, stock options are a critical tool for attracting the best managers, scientists, engineers and other creative individuals.

The same concern about excessively regulating stock options also applies to larger, more mature companies. In order to compete in the global economy, these multinational firms have to hire the very best, and one of the most effective ways to attract top-level talent is by providing incentives such as stock options. These same companies also invest tens and hundreds of millions of dollars into developing new products, and they don't want to lose the engineers and scientists who have created these intellectual properties. Trust me: when you invent a breakthrough product, everyone in your industry wants to steal it, and barring that, they want to steal the people who created it. Stock options are an effective tool for retaining these inventors and creators.

Eliminating or restricting stock options will only handcuff business even more without getting to the root of the problem. I believe we should consider something much simpler: we should bar top executives of public companies from cashing in their stock options until a minimum length of time has elapsed after they've left the firm—about eighteen months—and only after they've undergone a full, independent audit. This would ensure that they wouldn't be rewarded for actions that damaged the firm's profitability and slashed the value of every other investor's stockholdings. If the books were cooked, if there was any financial impropriety, it would bubble to the surface within a year. In other words, senior managers should be required to undergo a vesting period after leaving the company before being able to sell their shares.

This vesting rule would apply, at a minimum, to the chief executive officer, the chief financial officer and the chief operating officer of the corporation, and to other individuals as designated by the audit committee of the board. The days of bigwig executives bolting with all of the gold would quickly come to an end. Creating a vesting period would also motivate outgoing senior executives to be more diligent about succession planning, ensuring that first-rate managers would be filling their shoes after they've left the company.

Properly run, public companies are of immense value to society, because they allow a greater number of people to participate in the creation of wealth. And companies with dual-class share structures, such as Magna had before I sold operating control, are especially valuable to entrepreneurs looking to raise growth capital while still keeping a firm grip on the company they've nurtured. In Canada, the dual-class or multiple voting share structure has enabled the creation of a number of world-class companies over the years, including Rogers, Bombardier, Power Corporation, Telus, and Quebecor, to name just a few.

But corporate governance experts are fairly unanimous in their disdain for publicly traded companies with a dual-class share structure. So too are the big pension funds and investment firms. They are no longer content to be passive investors. They increasingly want to have a say in running companies, and that's simply not possible when a company has a dual-class share structure, as Magna did when I was chairman and controlling shareholder. And as a result, these investors are becoming more hostile and aggressive.

Before I stepped down as chairman at Magna and MI Developments, Magna's former real estate division, the battles between me and some of the big pension funds grew more and more acrimonious. It was emotionally and mentally taxing. Former Ontario premier Mike Harris, one of Magna's directors, brokered the deal with Magna's shareholders that saw me give up operating control in exchange for cash and stock. He was simply trying to facilitate what many Magna shareholders wanted: an end to the dual-class structure. But the pension funds were outraged by the settlement I received, even though shareholders voted overwhelmingly in favour it. They were looking to pin the blame on someone, and they made Mike the fall guy. They took out their wrath on him a year later by forcing him off the board after years of loyal and valuable service on behalf of shareholders.

When the pension funds and hedge funds took runs at me, it often got personal. One Wall Street hedge fund manager compared me to Fidel Castro at an MI Developments shareholder meeting because of the operating control I had through the dual-class share structure. But every investor knew the score going in. If they didn't like it, they should have invested their money elsewhere. I never broke the rules and operated strictly within the legal framework that was laid down. What's more, every legal challenge that was launched against me was dismissed or defeated.

In the late 1970s, I gave up a sizeable portion of my Magna stock in exchange for operating control, and in return I put in place the Corporate Constitution and the Fair Enterprise principles that fuelled Magna's explosive growth in the decades to follow. If it weren't for the dual-class structure, Magna would never have become the company it is today. It probably would have been swallowed up, splintered apart or run into the ground. The dual-class structure gave it the elbow room and financial oxygen it needed to grow, and a lot of people reaped economic rewards along the way.

YOU CAN'T FENCE IN MONEY AND TALENT

The reality of today's global economy is that virtually no nation or state can fence in people with great talent or wealth. The most highly skilled and creative people in the fields of science, art, sports and business—people whose talents are in great demand—are able to live and work anywhere in the world. And we can't blame talented people for moving to countries where they can make more money. The same is true of businesses. That's why countries in the developed world must be much more innovative in terms of creating a good business environment so that our best people and most successful businesses remain here at home.

CHAPTER 25

BETTING ON THE PONIES

All of us have what you might call a gambling gene.

M
agna Entertainment Corporation, or MEC for short, was the name I gave the company I founded in the late 1990s that included some of North America's most illustrious racetracks: Santa Anita Park, known the world over as the "Great Race Place"; Pimlico Race Course, home of the legendary Preakness Stakes, the middle jewel in the Triple Crown of racing; Golden Gate Fields, on the waterfront of San Francisco Bay directly across from the Golden Gate Bridge; and Gulfstream Park in Florida, which we would turn into a Sunshine State entertainment destination complete with a casino with 850 slot machines, upscale shopping and dining, and ocean-view condo developments.

Our racetracks annually hosted some of the richest and most prestigious racing events in the industry, including the Sunshine Millions, an MEC-branded event that pitted Florida-bred and California-bred horses against one another in a day-long racing extravaganza. We also introduced a lottery-type wager that gave racing fans the opportunity to win up to $500,000 in guaranteed prizes, a life-changing payout that you simply couldn't get through the traditional win, place and show bets on horse races.

We were a global gaming company, exporting our exclusive racing content to a worldwide audience via satellite, cable and the Internet. Our customers were able to wager on live racing either online or by phone through our Xpressbet division in the U.S. and our MagnaBet division in Europe. We formed an alliance with our main competitor, Churchill Downs Incorporated, owners of the famed Kentucky Derby, to jack up Internet wagering revenues by combining our horse racing content. More content equalled more races, and more races equalled more bets. We broadcast our races to 15 million subscribers through our HRTV cable and satellite television network, one of the world's leading producers of televised horse racing programming, creating shows from our TV studios in Los Angeles. We even owned the company that made the betting machines and wagering software through which our fans placed their wagers.

But in March 2009, after losing money for a string of years, MEC filed for bankruptcy. It was a crushing blow to me.

The MEC saga started with the acquisition of Santa Anita Park in 1999. When the racetrack first opened in the dirty thirties, nestled at the foot of the spectacular San Gabriel Mountains in sunny southern California, its stands were filled with racing fans, everyone from movie stars such as Cary Grant and Lana Turner to the down-and-out hoping to turn a long-shot bet into some winnings. And when we bought it in the late 1990s, the "Great Race Place" was still one of the shrines of thoroughbred racing.

The first time I ever went to Santa Anita Park was when I shipped my champion thoroughbred Glorious Song there to take part in a big-money stakes race back in the late 1970s. I couldn't even get into the Director's Room, the fancy lounge and restaurant overlooking the racetrack, because I didn't have a tie. I told myself that if I ever happened to buy the track one day, I would change that policy. And sure enough, I did. When Magna bought Santa Anita Park, one of the first things I did was to get rid of the requirement that ties had to be worn in the Director's Room.

I had always had my eye on Santa Anita Park. With its Art Deco architecture and panoramic vistas, it was one of the most stunning racetracks in the world. The first time it came up for sale, I sent a due diligence team down to scout it out, but I pulled the team once we learned the asking price would be astronomical. The racetrack ended up being sold to Meditrust, a health care and real estate investment trust, for approximately $450 million. But then about a year later I got a call from the investment bankers who had worked on the Meditrust deal. They asked me if I was still interested because Meditrust was in a cash bind and needed to sell Santa Anita quickly. I told the bankers to let Meditrust know that I wouldn't get involved in an auction, but if the price was reasonable, I could do the deal in a matter of weeks. One of the bankers called me back the next day. The price tag: $126 million. "It's a deal," I said.

Both Magna's management and board of directors were highly skeptical at first. But once they flew down to L.A. to see the track, and learned about the fire-sale price, they began to see the merit in owning the property, if only for the value of the real estate: 305 acres of highly desirable, prime development land on the edge of downtown Los Angeles. The way I saw it, branching into gaming and entertainment would allow us to diversify and create a second economic base. The main concern of management and the board, however, was the reaction of Magna shareholders.

The Magna purchase of Santa Anita Park sparked a firestorm in the investment world, and some of Magna's largest institutional investors were up in arms. At the annual shareholder meeting, I acknowledged their concerns: when investors buy automotive stocks, they don't want ponies thrown into the mix as well. So in February 2000 Magna made a binding commitment to shareholders that we would not put another penny of additional funding into MEC without their approval. The Forbearance Agreement, as it was known, was a kind of financial firewall around Magna, assuring shareholders of the automotive parts company that none of Magna's profits would get siphoned away into the gaming business. We lived up to the terms of agreement.

A month later, we turned MEC into a public company and spun it out by distributing MEC stock to Magna shareholders, who were then free to sell the stock or tuck it away in their portfolios. Magna shareholders ended up pocketing a nice return on the sale of their MEC shares. Following that, MEC became a separately traded public company controlled by Magna. A few years later we spun out the real estate division, MI Developments (MID), and Magna transferred its controlling interest in MEC to MID, which had the same dual-class share structure as Magna, with me as the controlling shareholder. It was the start of a bitter and protracted war between a number of MID shareholders, primarily hedge fund companies, and me. The hedge fund companies were only interested in the secure and steady income stream from MID's rental properties, and they lobbied hard for MID to

The Torrero, Magna's first concept vehicle, was unveiled in 1989 and still looks futuristic today, more than twenty years later.

Frank celebrates the successful launch of the Saab 9-3 Convertible at Magna's assembly factory in Graz, Austria, in 2003.

Magna workers in 2010 assemble the Aston Martin Rapide, the luxury sports car featured in a number of James Bond movies.

Each year, Frank would meet with randomly selected employees from Magna divisions throughout Canada and the U.S. to discuss issues that mattered most to them. This annual "Face to Face with the Chairman" session was a Magna tradition for more than two decades.

Frank and Belinda Stronach field employees' questions at an annual "Face to Face with the Chairman" session together with Marc Neeb, executive vice-president, Global Human Resources (*to the right of Frank*) and Don Walker, chief executive officer of Magna (*far right*).

Frank with Magna employees from across
North America at an annual shareholder
meeting.

Frank onstage with host Alex Trebek (*left*), at a taping of *Canada's Next Great
Prime Minister*, a program he created in 1995 to inspire young Canadians to
become involved in shaping the future of their country. The program gave
youth a national platform to share their ideas for building a better, stronger
and more prosperous Canada.

Frank (shown with Don Harron, a.k.a. Charlie Farquharson, *right*) has supported a number of children's charities over the years, including the Easter Seals organization, which raises money for children and young adults with physical disabilities such as cerebral palsy.

Frank officially opens the Magna Baltimore Technical Training Center for young African-American men and women in inner-city Baltimore who wish to pursue a career in manufacturing. Paul Myles (*centre right*), general manager of the facility, grew up in the neighbourhood where the training centre is located.

Frank led a dramatic rescue operation for victims of Hurricane Katrina in 2005, airlifting several hundred evacuees from New Orleans to a safe haven in Florida.

Frank started the annual Wild Wild West Hoedown as a barbecue fundraiser in his backyard. The event has since become one of the local area's largest annual fundraisers, drawing thousands for a festive night of country music.

Frank and Belinda Stronach present a cheque for more than $500,000 for twenty local charities and community groups at the 2010 Wild Wild West Hoedown. The annual event has raised more than $5 million over the years.

Elfriede and Frank Stronach accept the Queen's Plate from Queen Elizabeth II after their horse Awesome Again rode to victory in 1997.

Frank and Elfriede in the winner's circle after their horse Ghostzapper won the 2004 Breeders' Cup.

Andy, Elfriede and Frank Stronach accept the 2005 Eclipse Award for leading breeder from TV talk show host and horse racing aficionado Larry King.

Frank and former U.S. president Bill Clinton at Pimlico Race Course to watch the annual running of the Preakness Stakes.

Frank and U.S. secretary of state Hillary Clinton tour a Magna facility in New York.

Frank and former Canadian Auto Workers' (CAW) president Buzz Hargrove sign the historic Framework of Fairness agreement, making management and the CAW partners in ensuring productivity and fairness in the workplace.

NICK PERSICHILLI

Former U.S. president George H. W. Bush together with Frank and former Florida governor Jeb Bush.

Frank and Andy Stronach at the family stables.

Frank at his family farm in Aurora, Ontario.

cut MEC loose. I didn't realize it at the time, but it would become one of the factors that dragged MEC under in the end.

Around the time I formed MEC, the horse racing industry was fragmented, with tracks typically owned and operated by a lone individual or corporation. In a world where industries where consolidating, the horse racing business was stuck in time. As a leading racehorse owner, I raced at virtually all of the top tracks in America. And I was always amazed at how poorly they were run. There was no marketing pizzazz, many of the facilities were rundown and in dire need of a facelift, and the customer service was crummy. To make matters worse, the industry had failed to keep pace with advances in technology and changing customer preferences. It was no wonder horse racing was losing ground to alternate forms of gaming. But I thought it presented a powerful and potentially lucrative untapped business opportunity.

I believe all of us have what you might call a gambling gene. Whether it's playing a game of poker with your buddies, buying a scratch-and-win lottery ticket or taking a flyer on a penny stock that looks poised to shoot up in value, most people like to place bets and make wagers—whether it's for the pursuit of financial gain, for the satisfaction of picking a dark-horse winner or for the sheer excitement that comes with placing a bet and putting some money on the line. Standing at a slot machine is nowhere near as exciting as betting on the ponies and the adrenaline rush that comes with cheering your horse across the finish line. But the casinos and lotteries and other gaming businesses were doing a much better job of marketing their products.

With the poorly run racetracks, the rot usually started at the top. The track management and directors had a ritzy lounge, with gourmet food, expensive booze and cigars—you name it. When you spoke to them about the business, they thought everything was wonderful, all wine and roses. Hardly any of these racing executives ever went down to the grandstand to eat the tasteless burgers and hot dogs or drink the overpriced draft beer. But why would they care? In many regions of the country, they were the only game in town, and enjoyed what amounted to a monopoly. That's what happens whenever you have a monopoly—service deteriorates, the quality is shoddy, and the prices are sky-high. Monopolies are a curse on society.

MEC's vision was to bundle together some of the world's best horse racing content and make it available to a global audience through the Internet and satellite TV. But to do that, we had to assemble a critical mass of racetracks from coast to coast under the umbrella of a single company. By doing so, we determined that we could immediately achieve some economies of scale—everything from the costs of soft drinks to liability insurance. In practice, it didn't always work out that way. The highly fragmented regulatory framework often prevented us from standardizing operating practices or business models. It was like quicksand: the harder we kicked, the more we thrashed, the faster we sank.

The biggest mistake I made with MEC was to underestimate all of the rules and regulations that governed the sport and the impact on our bottom line that they would have. The hodge-podge patchwork of rules was laid down nearly a century ago, when wagering on horses was the only form of legalized gaming. The excessive regulations and outdated rules were the main reason, in my mind, the industry had declined so much since its heyday.

We were saddled with regulations that no other industry has to contend with, including dictating how many days of the year we could open our doors for business. Obviously, governments have a role to play in regulating all forms of betting in order to protect the public and uphold the integrity of the sport.

I met with countless governors and legislators from the states where our tracks were located, and I always had the same message: give our industry the opportunity to grow and compete according to the same free enterprise principles that govern other industries. I argued that racetracks should be treated like any other business—free to establish their own hours of operation and free to give customers the ultimate say in determining the success of a business. That way, the good racetrack operators will prosper and the bad ones will go out of business. When governments start telling you when you can open the doors of your business, you're in trouble. And we were in trouble. Despite massive lobbying efforts, both on our own as well as through various industry associations, we were largely unable to change any of the antiquated regulations. In the meantime, the losses kept mounting.

I always saw MID, MEC's parent company, as a financial cushion or backstop that would allow MEC to sustain losses in the early going until the fledgling racetrack company could get on its feet financially. Regardless of what happened on the racing side of the business, MID held all of the land the racetracks sat on. It was rock-solid collateral: hundreds of acres of prime, undeveloped real estate in major urban markets throughout the U.S. But MID shareholders, particularly the hedge funds, didn't see it that way, and we repeatedly locked horns.

When MID and MEC went public, the information circulars sent to prospective shareholders clearly spelled out that I had the controlling bloc of shares in both companies. Shareholders knew the score. But despite that, some shareholders alleged I had acted unfairly and launched legal action against me. The legal attacks were dismissed, but they were an enormous drain on my time and energy. I always had one eye on the litigation instead of both on running the business.

Our revenues climbed year after year but we couldn't turn a profit. A lot of money was lost. Even to the very end, we kept pouring cash in to keep MEC afloat. I truly felt sorry for the people who lost money. I knew of trainers and other people at the racetrack who had invested $1,000 or more in the stock—a lot of money for them. They believed in the business, and the money they had sunk into MEC was gone. I also believed the business could be viable, and I did everything I could to save MEC, but it was not to be. In the end, I personally lost more than any other single investor—about $40 million.

When MEC was finally pushed into Chapter 11 bankruptcy proceedings, I had no idea what fate lay in store for the racetracks. But once I sold operating control of Magna, I stockpiled enough cash to rescue the racing business. Otherwise, in all likelihood, the racetracks would have been pieced off or shut down, and the land they sat on sold to developers. I settled with MID's disgruntled shareholders—they got control of MID and were able to turn it into a pure real estate investment play, and I got the beleaguered racing assets. I acquired Santa Anita Park, Gulfstream Park, Pimlico, Laurel Park, Golden Gate Fields and some other racing-related businesses and properties and folded them into my privately held company, The Stronach Group. By the end of 2011, we had stopped the bleeding and finally turned a corner in terms of the profitability of the tracks. With MEC, we had simply run out of money, and we had run out of time.

I still believe that the business of horse racing has a great future. I'm free now to do a number of things that I couldn't do when MEC was controlled by MID.

From the beginning of recorded history, people have always bet on horse races. And I believe they always will.

LEAD BY EXAMPLE

My philosophy has always been that employees don't work for you—they work with you. I remember many times during the early years of my business when we would work late into the night to meet a deadline; I would roll up my sleeves and work on a bench alongside everyone else. There is no better way to lead than by example.

CHAPTER 26

THE HIGHER A MONKEY CLIMBS . . .

*The world is full of critics, but there are very few people who can offer
solutions.*

I'm pretty philosophical when it comes to all the criticism
I've received over the years. There's an old Caribbean saying that goes "The higher a monkey climbs up the tree, the
more his ass is exposed."

I used to face a lot of my critics in person each year at the
annual shareholder meetings of the various companies that I
chaired. One of my toughest critics—and also biggest support-
ers—was Denise Altman, a shareholder of Magna International
who came to our annual meeting each and every year well into
her eighties. She never pulled any punches, and if she thought
that we were falling short or going off course, she let us know.
But she was also the first to stand up and congratulate us on a
job well done.

Some of the criticism I've received over the years is about
the pay I make. I used to say that I should get paid as much as a

Hollywood actor, since I sometimes have to act on stage, and I should get paid at least as much as a professional hockey player, since I sometimes have to pass the puck. But the plain fact is, my pay is tied to Magna's profitability. The more profit Magna makes, the more I get paid. I don't know many executives who would base their compensation entirely on the performance of the company.

In 1990, when Magna didn't make a profit, I earned a base salary that was lower than the salary paid to some of our firm's junior lawyers. I can guarantee you that no one came rushing forward to say that Stronach should get paid more. I once told a shareholder who criticized my pay at an annual meeting that my employees are not only happy about how much I make— they hope I make even more the next year because that means that they'll also get more profit sharing. That's the Magna way, the Magna formula for success. There were several hundred employees in the crowd, and they broke out into spontaneous, thunderous applause.

The key point concerning management compensation is that it's primarily based on the profitability of the company. When Magna didn't make a profit in 1990, executive management—including myself—received compensation that was far below industry standards. At many companies, however, management is paid regardless of how the company performs. But if executive management steers the company in the right direction and Magna makes higher profits, then management, investors and employees all get a larger share of those profits. Everybody benefits.

Without good management, a company can't thrive. And you won't have good management unless you're able to attract the best in the industry by offering competitive wages and built-in performance incentives. The top managers are usually individuals who are capable of running their own business. If they could make more by running their own business, there would be no incentive for them to stay at Magna. So we need to make sure that we have the best people available, and we do this by providing incentives.

I look at some of the highest paid executives in North America—the hedge fund managers and investment bankers—and many of them didn't create a single job. It used to be that the more jobs you created, the more sales and profits you generated, the more money you made. But that doesn't seem to be true anymore. In today's business world, it seems that the more people you lay off, the more plants you close and jobs you kill, the more money you make. And I think we've got it backwards: the business leaders or executives we should really reward are the ones who create jobs and produce a profit.

Over the last few years, Magna absorbed a lot of criticism from pension funds and investment firms that our corporate governance practices were below standard. Some of the most vocal critics have been the large institutional investors, which tend to be concerned primarily with short-term profits. Lately, a lot of these institutional investors want to go beyond mere investing—they want to also have a major say in how the company is run. They're great at pumping up a stock's value, then flipping it, or stripping out the most valuable assets of a company and selling them for short-term gains, even if it damages the long-term viability of the business. And if laying off employees can boost short-term profitability—even if the company is doing well—they'll do it.

At a shareholder meeting a few years ago, a representative from one of those large institutional investors stood up and read a long criticism of Magna's dual-class structure—something they were fully aware of when they purchased our stock. I believe the investment firm had done quite well, since Magna had just posted record profits and sales, and the stock was up year over year. So I told the institutional investor: "You know, you guys remind me of the couple that buys a house next to the airport, and then constantly complains about the noise from the airplanes."

Ontario Teachers' Pension Plan (OTPP), which represents about 180,000 elementary and high school teachers in the province of Ontario, was an especially vocal critic despite the fact that it only owned a few shares in Magna. OTPP, most famous at one time for its ownership of the Toronto Maple Leafs hockey franchise, is a self-proclaimed crusader for good corporate governance, and it regularly lectures many of the companies it invests in on the topic of corporate governance. And although the OTPP always preaches about shareholder democracy, it curiously does not allow its own members to directly elect the board of directors. Those directors are appointed by the Ontario government and by the Ontario Teachers' Federation. The teachers, the ones who kick in all the money, have no direct say in how their money is invested.

For an organization that tells everyone else how to run their affairs, it can't seem to manage its own. As of the beginning of 2012, the Plan reported a shortfall of almost $10 billion. If this doesn't change, the Plan won't have enough money to cover the estimated future pension costs for all of the teachers when they retire.

Furthermore, a portion of the Plan's annual returns gets eaten up by the overhead associated with administering and managing the fund. (The fund employs more than 800 people.)

The fund managers are well paid and receive bonuses—even in years when the fund loses money.

What I've found is that the pension funds that complain the loudest about corporate governance are usually the ones with the worst corporate governance policies. The shareholders of these pension funds are workers—steelworkers, bricklayers, nurses, government administrators and teachers. And these workers have little or no say in how their retirement savings are managed. In essence, the workers have been disenfranchised by the massive pension funds that are the custodians of their life savings.

Magna's commitment to its shareholders is clearly spelled out in the Corporate Constitution, which gives investors a number of rights, including the guarantee that they could elect additional directors if Magna did not return a minimum threshold of profit. As it turns out, investors who stuck with Magna over the years made a lot of money. And any investor who didn't like the way we ran the company was free to sell his or her shares and invest elsewhere. That's not the case for the tens of thousands of Ontario teachers who are counting on OTTP to manage their pension savings.

Over the years, I've taken potshots from many different groups, everyone from organized labour and Wall Street investors to politicians and reporters. And during that time, I've been the subject of a lot of media coverage. Most of the reporting was fair and balanced, which is all that anyone can ask for, but some of it was shoddy and downright malicious. Most reporters mean well—they strive to perform their job to the best of their abilities; they want to accurately reflect what you're saying and report the news as objectively as possible. Some reporters, though, harbour a strong personal bias, either against a certain individual or against business in general. And these reporters will sometimes distort information or leave out key facts in order to paint a negative picture of a company or particular person.

I should state upfront that I believe the media is one of the main pillars of our society. It plays a vital role in informing citizens and serving as a check and balance on the activities of business and government. It can also have an enormous influence on reforming government and on educating citizens about important socio-economic issues or making them aware of problems that need to be addressed. In short, the media can be a positive force within our society.

I furthermore believe that a free press is a cornerstone of a free and democratic society. But that freedom shouldn't be a licence to publish inaccurate statements or falsehoods without any responsibility for the repercussions or consequences. A poison pen can do more damage than bullets. If the media doesn't do its homework, if it gets the facts wrong in a way that damages personal or corporate reputations, then it should be held liable.

Put it this way: if Magna ever made a faulty brake pedal and someone got injured as result, Magna would be penalized by the courts and sued for damages. But when media outlets damage reputations because of false reporting, there are hardly ever any serious financial penalties imposed.

The media believes that one of its chief roles is to hold business, government, academia and others to account through intense scrutiny and the constant monitoring and reporting of their activities. But who is reporting on the reporters? Who is holding the media to account? In the final analysis, the same tough standards the media uses to hold others to account must also apply to the media itself.

At this point in my life, I need more criticism like I need a hole in the head. If I wanted to, I could sit back, rest on my laurels, keep quiet and I would be in everyone's good books. But that would be taking the easy way out. I'm financially independent and not beholden to any individual or group. I don't need government handouts, and I don't have to cater to any politicians. I've always done what I thought was right and what I felt was in the best interests of my company and its stakeholders or the country and its citizens.

And if I really believe in a certain cause or issue, if I think something isn't right or fair, or if I think we're heading in the wrong direction, then you can be sure that I'll speak out.

TAKE PRIDE IN DOING SOMETHING WELL

My trade apprenticeship taught me to take pride in everything I do, no matter how small the job. If you don't possess the pride to do something well, and if that pride isn't deeply engrained in you, then you're doomed to mediocrity in whatever you do, whether it's your career or your business.

CHAPTER 27

MAKING THE WHEEL A LITTLE ROUNDER

If things don't function properly, be it in your personal life, in your business or in your country, you should know that you've got a problem. If you don't know that you've got a problem, then you've really got a problem. And problems are like cancer: if left unattended, they will grow.

As far as I'm concerned, making a better product for a better price isn't just a formula for making car parts. I've always believed that we should apply that thinking to every facet of society, especially those areas that have the greatest bearing on our quality of life: the economy, education and health care.

The truth is, the world is full of critics, but there are very few people who come forward with constructive solutions, and then submit those solutions to public scrutiny. Over the years, I've tried to do that, and I've encouraged others to do so as well.

There's nothing fancy about a lot of the ideas that I've put forward. I think they're fairly logical and based on fairness and common sense. Most importantly, I think they're ideas that could benefit everyone in society, not just a select few.

Competition in its purest form is what sports is all about. I love competition because it sharpens your mind, your senses, your body. Whenever I play tennis, I always want to square off against better players, because I end up improving my own skills and my own game.

We need to do more to develop what I call a "sports character" in students. Schools ought to devote more time to sports activities and other athletic endeavours. This will require building more facilities to give youth the venues they need to play and practise these various sports, but the long-term social and economic benefits would far outweigh the initial costs. Through an enhanced focus on sport, we would expose young people to the joys and rigours of competition, and this in turn would help them develop many desirable social qualities such as leadership, determination, teamwork, persistence and the harnessing of individual talent in the pursuit of a common goal.

The idea of making physical activity and athletic competition a key feature in the education of our youth is not a new one—it goes back to the classical civilizations of ancient Greece and Rome. But it seems as if we have recently lost sight of the tremendous virtue that comes with having a strong athletic component in our educational system. We need to return to those roots and begin reaping once again the many benefits that come through athletics and competitive sport.

In other words, I think we need to look at the many non-academic aspects of education that help develop well-adjusted citizens who will contribute to our social and economic well-being later in life. I call this approach "lifestyle education"—the teaching of basic principles that will enable young people to lead healthy, balanced and productive lives. Within the schools themselves, we need to place a much heavier emphasis on physical fitness and nutrition, particularly in the younger grades. Physical fitness and nutrition go hand in hand—they are the building blocks in the development of healthy young adults. Every child should have at least one nutritious meal at the school cafeteria or lunchroom, and the education system should instill an understanding of nutrition at an early age.

Students also need to acquire a greater awareness of how important the economy is to the overall functioning of our society, and we need to place a much greater emphasis in our school system on the creation of wealth—the underpinning of our living standards. I believe there's an anti-business bias in some quarters of our educational system. For some teachers and educators, "business" is a dirty word, and they hold the view that if a business does well, it must be because the company is taking advantage of people or engaged in unethical practices. For others, there are plenty of real-world examples to point to—companies that treat employees unfairly, or break the law or harm the environment. When that happens, it's not surprising that some people develop an anti-business disposition. And there are many teachers who absorb negative stereotypes through the media and movies. These negative stereotypes sometimes dissuade young people from thinking about careers in business, especially as entrepreneurs. But no matter how you slice it, students need to gain a greater understanding of the importance of business. If the economy doesn't function, nothing else will function either. Our health care, our education, our arts and entertainment, our social welfare systems—they all feed off the wealth that business creates.

We also need to promote technical education much more than we currently do. A college or university education is not for everyone. From ages 16 to 18, our students should be exposed to a wide range of trades, everything from carpentry and electronics to computer repair and automotive mechanics. When you look at the strongest economies in the world, Germany is always front and centre. And one of the reasons Germany is such a robust exporter of world-class products is that it places a lot of emphasis on engineering, on making products, and it can do this because of the country's outstanding trade and technical skills training.

In 2011, I received an honorary PhD in business administration from Laurentian University. I was greeted at the convocation ceremony by Jean Chrétien, the former prime minister, who teasingly called me "Dr. Stronach." Sitting on the stage, waiting to receive my honorary degree, I looked out at the hundreds of young university graduates in their caps and gowns, filled with hope and optimism, and I couldn't help but feel sorry for them given the state of the economy and their future prospects. Many no doubt incurred a lot of debt to pay for their education. And many obtained liberal arts degrees that will be of little practical value and, in many cases, will not lead to a productive career. In short, they want to contribute to society, but I feel we've let them down by not giving them the right tools, by not providing the best paths to rewarding and successful careers.

Lastly, I feel that we need to do more in regard to teaching our young people how to become economically free. Most people desire personal freedom (the right to choose their own road to happiness) combined with economic freedom—what might also be called financial independence. It astonishes me that we don't do more as a society to encourage economic freedom among individuals or encourage businesses to promote profit and equity participation so that workers can become part owners in their places of employment and share in the company's financial success.

By reforming our educational system to incorporate some of these ideas, we could help create better citizens with the skills needed to prosper in the new global economy. It's our duty to give students the tools they need to create and compete, and to open them up to the limitless possibilities that lie within their reach. If we can do that, then we will have a much greater chance of ensuring our future prosperity.

We need to undertake similar reforms in the field of health care. To begin with, I believe that in a civilized society every person must have access to basic health care. I see no reason why a public system and private system could not co-exist. But private health care providers should be required to make between 20 to 30 percent of their billings available at government-prescribed public rates. This would relieve the enormous strain on financial and human resources under a system of government-provided health care while opening the field up to a greater number of health care providers. The key features of any system are competition and incentives. Without competition, and without incentives that reward the best and most efficient, any health care system is destined to slide into mediocrity: costs begin to spiral higher, while quality deteriorates.

I've also been a long-time advocate of pushing medical care into the workplace as a way to deliver better health care services at a lower cost. By bringing health care workers directly into the workplace to improve health care access and services for employees and their families, we could reduce the health care costs paid by employers, individuals and the government.

In the early 1990s, in the midst of a severe economic downturn, I proposed this concept to the Ontario government.

Under my proposal, corporate-managed health care services would be made available to Magna's employees in that province and to their immediate family members (spouses, children, parents and grandparents) and would be carried out with the consent of employees, who would remain free to seek medical care elsewhere if they wished. Employees would be required to take part in paid preventive health education in the workplace. And employees would also be involved in overseeing the management of the program through the appointment of advisory board members. This new health care model would have taken an enormous strain off the clinics and hospitals in the regions where most of Magna's employees live and work.

And we threw in a classic Fair Enterprise twist: we proposed that all of the stakeholders get a cut of the savings associated with health care efficiencies. Employees would share a chunk of the savings in the form of a cash rebate, while the company would divvy up almost half of the savings. A portion would go to the doctors and medical staff in the form of an efficiency bonus to reward the more efficient delivery of health care services, and about 10 percent would go into a medical emergency account—a sort of rainy day fund. Through the new corporate model for health care delivery that I proposed, I believe we could have slashed costs by up to 30 percent while improving services.

In every health care catchment area of a certain size (approximately 30,000 employees and their family members), Magna would have built a state-of-the-art medical diagnostic centre with X-ray and laboratory facilities, and equipment such as ultrasound diagnostic imaging and MRI scanners. The costs associated with the purchase and maintenance of this medical equipment would have been covered entirely by Magna.

We would have also established a program of preventive health care that would involve a minimum of ten hours per year of education and learning within the workplace for each employee. The preventive health care program would stress the benefits of adopting healthy lifestyle choices and greater personal responsibility for individual health and wellness.

To me, the proposed Magna health care model was a pure win-win proposition for all of the stakeholders involved. Under the proposal, doctors would be relieved of administrative expenses and guaranteed a built-in clientele, and they would be eligible for bonuses strictly tied to efficiency gains; Magna would have a healthier workforce and less absenteeism due to medical appointments; employees would have more convenient service and the ability to earn health care rebates; and society would benefit by delivering better health care at a much lower cost through a model that could be replicated by other large employers throughout the province.

The cash-strapped government of the day, which was running record deficits, was intrigued by our proposal and our suggestion to conduct a trial run of this new prototype of health care delivery. Perhaps it got cold feet, or perhaps other political priorities crowded this off the agenda, but it never came to pass. Magna has more recently revived the health care plan. Perhaps this time, with deficits soaring once again and an ageing population eating up more and more health care dollars, government will be keen to experiment with a model that promises better health care at a lower cost.

When you get right down to it, I'm a systems guy. It doesn't matter if it's a car system or the education system. I suppose it's the toolmaker in me, but in my experience, unless the system is right, unless bottlenecks are unclogged and hindrances flushed out, things just won't function. My old partner Tony Czapka used to tell me to get my head out of the clouds. But I can't help it: if I see a way to make something better, I have to sketch out a plan.

CREATE A CHAMBER OF CITIZEN REPRESENTATIVES

Government is the management team of a country, but its decisions are driven primarily by political reasoning. It's what I call the Achilles' heel of democracy. So how do we take the politics out of politics? By introducing a new Chamber (or House) of Citizen Representatives that would place the country's socio-economic welfare and long-term national interests ahead of political considerations or partisan views.

CHAPTER 28

SHARING PROFITS WITH SOCIETY

A business that does not generate a profit is no good to anyone.

When Hurricane Katrina struck, I was sitting in a hotel room in California, watching the images of destruction and desperate people on the evening news, and I was deeply affected by the television coverage of Americans suffering through one of the worst natural disasters in that country's history. It was early September 2005, and Hurricane Katrina had caused massive flooding and damage that left close to 1 million people homeless and in need of food and shelter. The images reminded me of my own experiences as a boy in Austria during the final days of the war. Those experiences can never be erased—they're burned right into the soul.

I got in touch with some of Magna's senior executives to discuss how we could help. At the time, Magna was well on the way to recording another year of record sales and profits. We were fortunate because the company had a lot of resources at its disposal that we could put toward a rescue effort. And unlike government agencies that were hamstrung by red tape and bureaucratic approvals, we could take decisive action. We hastily put together an emergency rescue plan to move hundreds of evacuees by bus and plane to Palm Meadows Thoroughbred Training Center near West Palm Beach, Florida.

The very next morning, a team from Magna was on the ground organizing supplies of food, water and clothing and arranging transportation for the evacuees. Working with the U.S. Army and Air Force, as well as the American Red Cross, Magna's team successfully evacuated 250 people.

One of those people was Harold Brooks, who lived in the Bywater District of New Orleans, just six blocks from the Mississippi River and close to one of the two main levees that broke, leading to the massive flooding that left hundreds of thousands of people homeless. Just before Hurricane Katrina reached shore, Harold made sure that his mother, his two sisters—one of whom is handicapped—and his nieces and nephew left town in the one car they all shared. Harold gave them the last few dollars he had for gas money.

After the hurricane flooded his home, the search-and-rescue operations were temporarily suspended and all water and gas were cut off. In the days that followed, Harold would make his way up and down the flooded streets, taking food to families who had been stranded in their homes and checking in on his neighbours. He remembers seeing bodies floating past him down the street and he told us: "I didn't look too close because I didn't want to see who it was." When he was rescued, Harold was wading through the flood waters, trying to coax a mother and her three children to come with him. The mother didn't want to leave her badly ruined home.

More than 1,000 volunteers, doctors, nurses and chefs were waiting at the Florida training facility to lend a helping hand as the New Orleans evacuees arrived. Among the evacuees were many families with small children, seniors and disabled people. Some were wearing nothing more than shoes and a blanket. Many were carrying all of their possessions in a garbage bag. Dennis Mills, a long-time Magna executive and friend, was directing the operation. Dennis was a wizard at mobilizing people to support a cause. About two years before Katrina struck, the SARS epidemic hit Toronto, killing dozens of people, and the World Health Organization issued an alarmist advisory urging people not to travel to the city, an edict that devastated the local economy. Dennis brought the Rolling Stones and some of the world's greatest rock bands to Toronto for a concert that was broadcast around the globe to show people that it was safe to come to the city. When I flew down to Florida and arrived at the site of the rescue operations, Dennis grabbed my arm and said, "Frank, what an unbelievable experience. I feel like I've just witnessed a miracle."

Feeding the evacuees and giving them temporary shelter was the easy part—finding a way to help them rebuild their shattered lives was much more difficult. One thing was certain: we were committed to seeing this through to the end. And to make that happen, we decided to purchase some land in Louisiana and build a community from scratch, giving the Magna evacuees the opportunity for a fresh start and a new life.

Shortly after the Magna evacuees settled in to Palm Meadows, I visited a 1,000-acre parcel of land in Simmesport, Louisiana, north of Baton Rouge. The site would become the future home for many of the Magna evacuees and other victims of Hurricane Katrina. My attitude regarding the evacuee assistance was simple and straightforward: Canadians and Americans are neighbours, and neighbours help one another.

Magna obtained building permits and ordered a number of manufactured homes. The homes were delivered to the Simmesport project site, providing comfortable and modest living accommodation for the displaced hurricane victims. Within a few days, the evacuees had christened their new home "Magnaville."

We then investigated a number of agricultural ventures for the rural community, including catfish and crawfish farming, as well as swine, poultry and cattle operations, all of which could provide food and a source of income. A number of other Canadian and U.S. corporations stepped up to the plate and contributed to the Simmesport Magnaville project, including construction firms Con-Drain and Giffels Corporation, architectural and engineering firm NORR Limited, and TerraNova Partners L.P., an investment fund. Organized labour chipped in too: Ontario's Carpenters' Union, representing more than 20,000 skilled tradespeople, helped with the construction of the homes. The union's leader, Ucal Powell, personally spent the better part of a month in Louisiana pounding nails and sawing two-by-fours to build porches for the prefabricated homes we set up on the property. The community was fully operational by early November and included a community centre and sports and recreation area. We also built a hurricane evacuation centre for the residents of Louisiana that has subsequently served as a safe house for people affected by a natural disaster.

When all was said and done, we felt responsible for the evacuees. They were Magna's adopted community. We made a five-year commitment to the project and saw it through to the end. During that time, a number of the residents learned new skills. Many got back on their feet and started new lives in New Orleans and in other parts of the United States. We gave them that chance.

On the heels of Hurricane Katrina came another natural disaster that galvanized the company into providing assistance. Only one month later, a devastating earthquake hit the north-western region of Pakistan, claiming the lives of close to 80,000 people. A large number of those killed were schoolchildren who had just started morning classes. I sent one of Magna's longest-serving employees from the corporate head office to investigate and see what we could do. Magna Training Manager Atta Mohammed, who started with Magna on the factory floor back in the 1970s, had immigrated to Canada from Pakistan. I asked him if he'd be willing to go to Pakistan on behalf of the company and find out how we could best help.

He visited the disaster site on behalf of Magna only days after the quake. Atta told me that he climbed down a gaping hole in the earth where an elementary school once stood and saw, scattered among the boulders and twisted steel, small back-packs and pencils. When he returned, we announced that we would donate money and assistance to help build a school in one of the worst-hit areas of the region.

The school is known as TCF School–Magna Campus in honour of the donation made by Magna and the support pro-vided by The Citizens Foundation, a Pakistani non-profit orga-nization. It's located in the village of Chir, close to the borders of Afghanistan and China. In 2012, the Magna Campus began its sixth year of operation, bringing hope and learning to more than 200 children in the poorest part of the country. What is particularly remarkable, especially in that part of the world, is that nearly half of the students are female. Most classes are taught in the local language, Urdu, while math and science are taught in English, which students begin learning in their first year.

The Pakistani school project and the New Orleans rescue mission were funded through the Social Responsibility principle contained in Magna's unique profit-sharing formula—a profit-sharing principle that has enabled Magna to support numerous charitable and social causes over the years.

I believe that all of us should, from time to time, look in the mirror and ask ourselves how we might be able to serve society. Back in the 1970s and 1980s, I volunteered for Big Brothers, a charity that matches adult male volunteers with boys who have no father. The Big Brother offers his "Little Brother" support, encouragement and guidance. As a Big Brother, I would take my Little Brother to sporting events or sometimes to the office where I worked. I enjoyed the time I spent with him—it made my heart feel good knowing that I might be a positive influence in his life. Like any volunteer, I gladly and freely gave my time and energy, without any expectation of payment or reward. That's the essence of the volunteer spirit. I used to joke that if the Big Brothers organization were run by the government, you might end up with a bureaucrat who'd say: "The pay's great but I hate spending time with the little bugger."

In addition to volunteering as a Big Brother, I've served as a volunteer board member over the years for numerous charitable, educational and philanthropic causes, including the boards of hospitals and universities. These experiences have given me valuable insight into the many needs and issues that exist in society. Not only do businesses have a responsibility to support the social fabric, but so too do individual citizens, especially those among us who are more fortunate and who have the means and opportunity to give back to society. And at Magna, giving back to society isn't about charity—it's about sharing profits with one of our key stakeholders, society.

That's one reason why Magna established a technical training centre a number of years ago in Park Heights, a crumbling inner-city neighbourhood in Baltimore, Maryland, plagued by high unemployment. One of our racetracks, Pimlico, home of the famous Preakness Stakes race, sat right next to Park Heights. One day I said I wanted to meet some of the community leaders to see if there was anything we could do to help the community. They were a little skeptical at first. No outsider—no politician, no business person, no philanthropist—had ever shown an interest in the neighbourhood. So we got in the car and drove up and down the streets. The place looked like a war zone: homes with shattered windows, graffiti and garbage, boarded-up buildings. One building in particular caught my attention: an abandoned elementary school. I inquired into whether or not we could get the school. My plan: turn it into one of the most modern technical training centres in the country.

But I needed someone to run the facility. So I checked into whether Magna had any managers with a strong technical background, someone who would be a good person to take young teens from the Park Heights neighbourhood and turn them into toolmakers. A couple of our operations people suggested Paul Myles, an up-and-coming Magna manager working in the Detroit area. I called Paul and asked him to come up and see me; I said I had an intriguing proposition. We chatted for a bit about business at his factory, and then I told him about our plans for a technical training centre. "Would you be interested in running it?" I asked. "Would I ever," he said. Incredibly, as fate would have it, Paul Myles grew up in Park Heights, a stone's throw from the location of the training facility. The idea of returning to his roots and giving kids in the neighbourhood the same shot in life that he had meant the world to him.

So in January 2005, with Paul Myles at the helm, the Magna Baltimore Technical Training Center opened its doors to young African-American men and women living in the area. It was state of the art, complete with the most technologically advanced equipment, as well as a gymnasium and community activity centre. I wanted to give the kids in the area hope, a ticket to a better life. At the official opening ceremony, a number of the neighbourhood residents had tears in their eyes.

We believe some of the future graduates will one day work for Magna—and perhaps become managers. To be a Magna manager, you've got to grasp the production process inside out, otherwise you cannot lead the men and women who work on the factory floor. The training program we launched in Baltimore has already changed lives, turning homeless youth living on the streets into skilled tradesmen earning a good middle-class wage.

We did something similar nearly twenty years earlier: building a Magna factory in a remote, economically depressed area. It was probably considered the last place on earth that Magna would ever build an auto parts factory.

In the late 1980s, we announced plans to open a manufacturing facility in Cape Breton, a harsh, rocky region of Canada that juts out into the Atlantic Ocean. Cape Breton was traditionally a coal-mining region, and most of the men who worked near Sydney, the largest town in the area, were coal miners. But the industry fell on hard times, a lot of the mines closed and the unemployment rate in the region was among the highest in the country.

The Canadian government had promised local residents

that it would bring new industry to the region and approached Magna about building a factory there. I was intrigued, because I believed in the notion that if you had the right business philosophy and the right operating principles, you could go into an economically depressed area and create a profitable business. It was, for me, an acid test for Magna's Fair Enterprise philosophy.

Geographically, it didn't make any sense—Cape Breton was thousands of miles from our closest customers. But there was another factor to consider, one that wasn't based purely on hard business costs. It was the question of whether or not we could make a contribution to society by creating manufacturing jobs in a remote region of the country.

I visited the area and immediately took a liking to the Cape Bretoners. They were salt-of-the-earth people: friendly, good-natured and industrious. Their families had been there for generations. And I thought they had won, through sheer toil and perseverance, the right to be given another chance. While the community was elated about the news that Magna would open a factory, some of our shareholders were less enthusiastic.

It was a seedling. And we left it to the people in that community to nurture that seedling with our help and oversight. The facility was around 100,000 square feet and had all of the most modern equipment. We even started a small program to train tool and die makers right in the plant. Many of the employees were the sons and daughters of coal miners.

The plant struggled in the early years. We tried to zero in on the right product, and decided to manufacture small transmission components—parts that could more easily be shipped long distances. And eventually, despite the predictions of many skeptics, the plant began to turn a profit in the early 1990s. But the Cape Breton facility, under pressure from cheaper suppliers in

Asia Pacific, saw profits sink. When the economic crisis hit and the auto industry ground to a halt, business all but dried up.

The facility provided meaningful work for many people for many years. We gave a lot of young people a good grounding in technical skills and trained a number of toolmakers—people who gained the know-how to create products and open their own small tool shop. The Cape Breton plant proved that with the right business approach, and with hard-working people willing to make the enterprise a success, a business could make a go of it, even in a part of the world that most people had written off.

Cape Breton and Park Heights are worlds apart but they share one thing in common: it's easy to count people out when they've been knocked down, but it's amazing what they will do when someone gives them a hand up and a second chance.

Whether in business or in society or in your own personal life, if something doesn't function properly, you should know that you've got a problem. And if you don't know that you've got a problem, then you've *really* got a problem. Problems are like cancer—they don't go away by themselves. They have to be identified and treated or they will grow. And the first step in identifying and treating them is speaking out.

One of the great dangers we need to be on guard against is citizens, especially young people, who become pacified to the point where no one any longer cares about trying to improve society, because everyone considers that to be the responsibility solely of the state.

We owe it to ourselves to stop sweeping problems under the carpet. We owe it to ourselves to stand up and speak out. That sentiment—the desire of regular citizens to fix what is wrong with the country—is what inspired me more than fifteen years ago to create a competition that asked college and university students to come up with solutions for making their country more prosperous.

It was called the Canada's Next Great Prime Minister program. Its mandate: to inspire young Canadians to become involved in shaping the future of their country, and to give them a national platform to share their ideas for building a better, stronger and more prosperous Canada. We were tapping into the ideas of ordinary citizens, the sort of discussion and debate you'd hear in a corner coffee shop or bar, with people saying, "If I were running the country, I'd . . ." And then they proceed to passionately tell you what they would do to make the country better.

The competition eventually evolved into a national TV show, complete with a panel of judges composed of former prime ministers and a live studio audience that votes for the contestant of their choice to become "Canada's Next Great Prime Minister." We ended up licensing the TV show concept to a number of countries around the world, including Germany, with ongoing interest from many others. Over the years the annual contestants have admirably addressed the problems facing their country with creativity, courage and conviction. A number have since gone on to become elected politicians.

In seeking a new vision for the future, it's only natural that we turn to young people. After all, no one has more at stake in the future than they do. The issues these students address, such as reforming the political system and igniting economic growth, are issues that will ultimately have a bearing on the country's standard of living. And who knows? Perhaps a future president or prime minister will have gotten their start as a contestant in this unique program.

What really fires me up to become a donor or volunteer is that it would eat away at my conscience to know that someone needed help and I did nothing about it. It's like the story of the teacher who takes his students on a field trip out into the country. They hear the distant whining and yelping of a dog. At first the teacher ignores the cries, but after a while, he follows the barking until he discovers a dog, trembling and exhausted, entangled in a leash tied to a tree. He unties the dog and one of the students congratulates him on his good deed, saying he was a kind man. The teacher replies that his conscience would have bothered him and he wouldn't have been able to sleep at night had he ignored the dog's cries for help any longer.

And so it is in life. Certain experiences become embedded in your soul, forever stuck in your mind. If I could enrich someone's life, make it better in even the smallest way, or if, through my actions or the knowledge I've accumulated, I could bring happiness to someone less fortunate, then I feel compelled to do so. But just giving money alone isn't the answer. Just as important—perhaps even most important—is what we can donate in terms of our time and talent.

The beauty of the profit-sharing formula I created at Magna is that a cut of the profits goes to society. Two percent may sound minuscule, but when profits approach the $1 billion mark, 2 percent is $20 million—money that gets invested into hospitals to buy advanced equipment for diagnosing and treating cancer and heart disease. It's money that is donated to local soccer and hockey teams to buy jerseys and scoreboards and pay for ice time and referees. And it's money that supports senior citizens, hospices for the dying, rehabilitation programs for wayward youth, and virtually every sort of charity and volunteer agency that helps individuals and families in need. That's the great thing about having a successful company—you can share that success with society by improving the lives of others.

There's not a day goes by that I don't think: *I am truly blessed.* Life's been great to me. I've had no real setbacks—no major sicknesses, no handicaps. I've got everything a man could want. With all of the resources at my disposal, I simply can't, in all good conscience, sit passively by when I have a chance to make things better. I look at my grandson and my granddaughters and all of our future generations and I think, *What kind of world do I want to leave behind? What contributions can I make so that we can have less poverty and a better society?* I've got to do what I can to change the system for the better.

GIVE BACK

I believe that all of us should, every now and then, reflect on how we might be able to serve society. For instance, I always tell students to remember that they're fortunate to have been given the opportunity to study, and that while they have a right to use that knowledge and training for their own personal benefit, they should never forget that some of the knowledge they've accumulated should also benefit society.

CHAPTER 29

THE HARDER YOU WORK, THE LUCKIER YOU GET

Some people have to clean the sewers, but as a society we must ensure that we never screw the sewer covers on so tightly that someone can't climb out and perhaps one day hold the highest office in the land.

O verall, I consider myself a pretty lucky guy.

Luck can play a role in many aspects of our lives. But at the same time, I've always believed that you have to try to influence the amount of luck that comes your way. It's like the old saying: You've got to be good to be lucky. And at the same time I also truly believe that opportunity often comes calling. You just have to be on the lookout for it.

Next to my Canadian home are the barns where a number of my thoroughbred racehorses are stabled. In the spring and summer, after visiting the barns in the morning, I usually walk through the grass on the way back to my house. The grass has large patches and clumps of clover throughout, which the horses love to eat. And often when I walk through the grass, I stop to see if I can find a four-leaf clover. According to popular tradition, the leaves bring good luck to their finders. I've even heard it said that there are 10,000 three-leaf clovers for every one four-leaf clover.

Maybe I'm more superstitious than I'd care to admit—or maybe I just enjoy the challenge—but you'll often find me at that time of the day, bent down, sweeping my hands through the grass, trying to spot that classic symbol of good fortune. Most days, I come up with a four-leaf clover—sometimes a whole bunch. I pick them out of the patch and scoop them up left and right: *bam, bam, bam.* And people who are with me usually say, "How can you do that? I can't see any." But to me, they jump out—it's as if they're red. It's not unlike when you immerse yourself in something—you start filtering out the noise that you don't want to hear, the objects you don't want to see. You start zeroing in and you get so close you can practically see the skeleton.

Whenever I have a bad experience, I try to take away a lesson so I don't make the same mistake again. But I never look back in anger. I don't get upset or hold grudges because that generates negative energy. It's also a question of being pragmatic: what's the point in getting mad? What are you going to solve? I always look ahead and stay positive. I'm happy with whatever I have, whatever hand I get dealt. I simply make the best of it. And I always try to see if I can take something and make it a little better.

I'm no different from most people. When things are going smoothly, when the sun is shining, I lay off the pedal a bit, slow down, become more playful. But when things are tough, I knuckle under. I shut out all of the diversions. And I really believe that from time to time a storm can be healthy. It tests you. It weeds out weaknesses and blows off the rotten branches. As long as it doesn't sink the ship, a storm can be a good thing.

I'm a true believer that in business—and in life—opportunity and good future often come disguised as hard work. One of my favourite Canadian writers is the humorist Stephen Leacock. What I admire most about Leacock is the way that he could weave certain timeless truths into a witty phrase or funny story. One of my favourite lines from Leacock's writing goes something like this: "I'm a great believer in luck—the harder I work, the more luck I have."

Leacock's famous quotation reminds me of a newspaper ad I once saw describing a lost dog. The ad said: "Missing. A black Labrador with a crippled leg. Was run over by a truck. Big scar on its back. Was shot by a hunter. Getting on in age and half-blind. Answers to the name of Lucky." Sometimes lately I feel like that old Labrador.

Other times I feel like the maple tree that stands in a field near the Magna head office property in Aurora. I've been told the tree, based on the size of the trunk, is probably more than 100 years old. Sometime during the 1980s the tree got hit by lightning. The lightning strike split the trunk in half and sheared off most of the tree. But a large limb growing close to the ground survived and has continued to grow.

A while back, a local artist asked for permission to come on the property and paint the extraordinary tree. The artist created a number of watercolour prints of the maple in fall, summer, spring and winter, and titled the series *Endurance*.

When construction was taking place on the property a number of years ago, I had a chain-link fence put up around the tree in case one of the workers on a bulldozer ripped it out by its roots, mistaking it for deadwood. I figured if the tree had made it this far, the least I could do was give it a fighting chance.

About three years ago, we were told by an arborist that the

tree would most likely not survive the winter. The core of the trunk was rotten and riddled with ants. But in spring, incredibly, the tree put out leaves once again. The decaying trunk was splitting apart, causing the last surviving limb to fall toward the ground, so we propped up the big branch with a handmade wooden truss. We then took seedlings—around forty or fifty—and we planted them all over my property.

I drive by the tree quite often on my way to the office, and I confess to having a soft spot for that old maple. You've got to admire its tenacity. It's been through a lot and seen a lot, and it has the scars to prove it. And just when you are ready to count it out, just when you think it's had about all it can take, it fights on, still full of life. I would like to think that tree and I share something in common.

I often say that when you're at the right place, at the right time, with the right sort of ingredients, a lot of great things can happen. And by ingredients I mean the experiences that you accumulate in life. When you've experienced hunger or deprivation or persecution, you're better able to sympathize with someone who has suffered.

When I look back now and analyze my life, I can see clearly that my early experiences growing up in Austria during the Depression and World War II contributed greatly to my success later in life. In the final analysis, I believe these experiences gave me the ability to recognize and seize opportunities that came along, and they taught me important lessons that I could apply to my career, first as an entrepreneur building my own business, and later as the CEO of a multinational corporation with employees and customers throughout the world.

But the ingredients—the experiences I gained along the way—were the intangible qualities that helped me to succeed whenever opportunities presented themselves. In other words, it's not enough to be at the right place and the right time— you must also have the right ingredients. Like most things in life, luck plays a role. So too does our education, our upbringing, our skills and talents. But what often makes the difference between success and failure are the experiences we bring to bear on the challenges and opportunities that present themselves.

I often get asked to state, in a few words or a short sentence, how I would like to be remembered long after I'm gone. And I usually answer: "He kept his word; he was fair; and most of all, he made a contribution to build a better society."

Magna, the name of the company I built from scratch from a one-man tool shop, is Latin for "great." It's not a name that I picked, but one that I inherited when I merged my young company with an electronics and aerospace manufacturer in the late 1960s. Nevertheless, the company has lived up to its name, growing in size and strength year after year, decade after decade, to the point where Magna today spans the globe, with more than 380 factories and R & D centres in twenty-six countries on five continents. Moreover, Magna is widely regarded as the world's leading company in terms of automotive technologies. That is a legacy I am proud of, and the creation of Magna is one of the lasting accomplishments that I would always like to be remembered for.

The same holds true for my activities in the horse racing business. I've bred some of the greatest horses in history. I've also tried to modernize the "sport of kings," and in the process I've generated some controversy along the way. Many of the people in the horse racing industry appreciate what I'm trying to do and support my efforts. But some have felt I was not respecting the industry's heritage and history, even if they recognized that the old ways were no longer working. Whatever happens, I hope that when the dust settles, the fans and the horsemen, the jockeys and the breeders, will all look back and say, "Stronach made a great contribution to racing."

If I had to name the accomplishment that I am most proud of, it would be the Fair Enterprise business philosophy I developed while at Magna. When I started out in business, I didn't have any grand philosophies—I was simply struggling to get the business off the ground and make enough money to cover my operating and living expenses. What I would later label as the Fair Enterprise philosophy—the entrepreneurial business principles that have shaped Magna's growth over the years—is something that evolved naturally from the way my business grew.

Fair Enterprise isn't just some ivory-tower theory that exists only in the pages of a pamphlet—it's a living, breathing operating philosophy that still guides the day-to-day operations of Magna's manufacturing facilities around the world. In essence, we've built a real-world role model—and I believe that any business that adopts our philosophy and follows in our footsteps can attain the same levels of extraordinary growth and success.

PURSUE EXCELLENCE

The desire to be the best and to pursue excellence is a powerful human urge. We need to be careful that we don't limit or shut off the avenues that allow people to get ahead and make a better life for themselves and their families. And we shouldn't pull down those who are trying to rise higher and reach the very top of their respective fields, whether it be business, science, academia or the arts. In the final analysis, any society that stifles individuals in the pursuit of productivity, ingenuity and creativity is a decaying society.

CHAPTER 30

RETURNING TO MY ENTREPRENEURIAL ROOTS

The reality is that people are not truly free unless they have economic freedom. It's a shame that only a small percentage of people are economically free. Our challenge, therefore, is to figure out how the majority of people can attain economic freedom.

I couldn't sleep. Anxious for the day to begin, reflecting on all that I had done in all the years gone by, I awoke at 4 a.m. It was May 6, 2010, and in a few hours, in the ballroom of a suburban Toronto hotel, I would announce that I had decided to sell operating control of Magna International Inc.

I had come to the decision to relinquish control after a great deal of reflection. The timing was right. And I felt it was the right thing to do. What's more, I was prepared to accept the verdict of the shareholders. If they rejected the offer, I would have remained the controlling shareholder. Either way, I would have been happy. Absorbed in thought, I lost track of time and ended up dashing out of the house and speeding down the highway to the hotel. In my haste, heading to the most important share-holder meeting of my career, I realized that I forgot to put on a tie. If my good friend Tony Czapka were still around, he would have smiled and said, "No more monkey suit for you, Frank."

When I addressed Magna stockholders for the last time as the controlling shareholder, I shared with them some of the soul-searching that led to my decision, and I shared as well some of my feelings surrounding this milestone event in my life. I had put a lot of real blood, sweat and tears into growing Magna into the company it is today, and I still know where pretty much every screw and bolt is located. I built an automotive powerhouse brick by brick, a company that is known and respected the world over. But the most important outcome for me is the fact that Magna now employs more than 110,000 people around the world. When you think of the spinoff or multiplier effect on the economy that all those jobs create, and when you count the family members who depend upon those jobs, the impact of Magna is enormous, touching the lives of several million people. It's a reality I was always keenly aware of as the founder and chairman—the knowledge that every decision I made could directly affect hundreds of thousands of people.

Magna will always be much more to me than just a business. So it wasn't an easy decision for me to sell control of the company I had nurtured. Why, then, did I sell control? First of all, I truly felt that the current rules and regulations governing public companies had become stifling, even strangling. I started to feel that I was operating with a straitjacket on, and every business decision down to the minutest detail had to be double-checked and rubber-stamped by lawyers and bureaucrats. All the thrill and zest that comes with building something bold and big was gone, sucked dry by the never-ending rules and regulations. Second, the horse racing business meant a great deal to me. By selling control of Magna, I was able to acquire sufficient funds to inject into the horse racing business to help it turn the corner and get it back on the path to prosperity. And lastly, I was never meant to be the chairman of a public company: I'm an entrepreneur at heart, a builder of businesses.

Looking back, I can honestly say that I have no remorse, no regrets. When I'm asked why I relinquished control, I often joke that I came to the realization that I couldn't manage Magna from the grave, as much as I'd want to. But the reality is I've put in place a system and a set of operating principles that are stronger than any one individual or group of people. They'll guide the company's future growth for decades to come. If Magna should ever stray from its founding principles, or abandon them altogether, then it will become just another company. And even though I won't be on the stage at future Magna shareholder meetings, there's one thing you can be sure of: I will always be available to give guidance if called upon, and I will always be there for the company I founded.

A reporter recently asked me how it felt now that I had stepped back from the business of running Magna. I replied, "What do you mean 'step back'? I'm busier than ever before."

My entrepreneurial zeal is as strong today as it was the day I opened the one-man tool and die shop. I have hundreds of ideas for new businesses, new products and new services. And in the years ahead, I intend to pursue a variety of ventures that I'm passionate about. Freed from the constraints imposed by the regulations governing public companies, I'll be able to run much faster, and with fewer strings attached. I'll be an entrepreneur once again.

I have nothing holding me back. I have the drive and desire. I have plenty of resources at my disposal. And I have one other ingredient that I lacked when I first started out: experience. I am smarter, wiser and more perceptive today than I was fifty years ago or even five years ago.

I'm eighty years young now, and I increasingly wonder, *When will I slow down?* The answer: probably when I'm confined in a box. In the meantime, I'll be incubating a number of innovative new products and businesses in health care, agriculture, real estate, retirement care, gaming and entertainment and electric technologies. It's like I'm standing on the deck of that old Dutch freighter in the Rotterdam harbour, as I did nearly sixty years ago, setting sail for a new world, nothing but a vast ocean of limitless possibility before me.

The money I've accumulated over the years won't be sitting in a bank either—I'll put it to work to launch new companies and create new jobs. The truth is, nothing compares to the sense of satisfaction that comes with building a business from the ground up and giving the people who work alongside you a piece of the action. That's what I will continue to do for many years still to come. I'll turn raw materials and ideas into tangible products that improve people's lives. I'll plow profits into the development of new medicines that heal and technologies that give millions of people the world over the freedom to travel. In the end, I'll do what I have always done: I will make a better product for a better price.

Behind my home, just past the horse barns, there's a spectacular forest filled with maple, birch and pine. Early mornings I enjoy going for a walk through the woods by myself with the sun rising behind the trees. I'm not an overly religious man but I sometimes stop and pause, marvelling at the splendour of nature, the dew sparkling on the grass like a thousand diamonds, and I say a silent prayer. I thank God for all the blessings I've received, and I hope that I can make a contribution to better the lives of people.

At this point in my life, I'm not looking for titles or honorary degrees or medals. I want to be of service to society. I want to make a lasting contribution, one that sets society on a new and positive course. I want to do my part to build a society that is more prosperous and more democratic, a society that has greater fairness and greater freedom. Most of all, I want to find ways of giving people the opportunity to pursue the same road to economic freedom that I followed.

BUILDING A BETTER AND MORE PROSPEROUS SOCIETY

The history of man has always been dominated by the Golden Rule: the person who has the gold makes the rules. I would never want anyone to dominate me or my children, and if I feel that strongly, then I should never expect to be able to dominate anyone else. The key is: we must dismantle the chains of domination—not via a destructive revolution, but via a revolution of the mind.

What would constitute an ideal society? It's a question that many people ask themselves, and one that people throughout the ages have grappled with. I know that in my case, especially as I get older and have a little more time to reflect, the question of what an ideal society might look like increasingly occupies my mind.

To begin with, society is made up of individuals, and therefore any conception or outline of an ideal society must start with an understanding of the hopes, dreams and aspirations of people. I'm not so presumptuous as to speak for all people, but I think I can safely speak for 99.99 percent of all people. I strongly believe that people, first and foremost, want to have individual freedom. If I had to summarize what that means, it would be this: let everyone choose their own road to happiness without preventing others from pursuing that same path. In Western societies, we have relatively good human charters of rights that protect individual freedom. But we also have to recognize that people aspire to be economically free. If you're not economically free, you're not really a free person, and it's a shame that so few people are economically free. That's why I also believe that societies must devise a framework that would enable a greater number of people to attain economic freedom.

But what does it mean to be economically free? In terms of Western society, I think people should be able, after having worked for twenty years, to own their own modest homes and have enough money in the bank to live a modest lifestyle on the interest income from their savings. They should be free to nourish their hearts, souls and minds by pursuing lifelong passions and hobbies, be they artistic pursuits or volunteering for a charity. In the final analysis, success in life can only be measured by the degree of happiness you achieve.

One of the great downfalls of business is that it has neglected turning workers into capitalists through profit and equity participation programs that would allow workers to accumulate enough capital that they could become economically free. Another problem that is growing in scope is that Western countries are more and more becoming financial economies instead of real economies—economies that make products. You can see how far we have drifted away from a real economy by walking down the aisles of any major department store and seeing that hardly any of the products on the shelves are made in North America or Europe. And one of the main reasons for this is that companies in the West are rewarded via the tax system for clos-ing factories and shifting their manufacturing to Asia. It should be the other way around: companies that invest their profits in their home country, creating jobs and spending money on new machinery and R & D, should be rewarded by not having to pay any tax.

The current tax structure is not conducive to manufacturing. When you look around, wherever new buildings are springing up, they are seldom factories; they are increasingly warehouses for products made in Asia. When a country imports more and more and exports less and less, the economy will deteriorate, causing massive unemployment.

History teaches us that societies come and go. When the economy breaks down, it is only a matter of time before society as a whole begins to unravel. That's one of the main reasons I am launching a new policy think tank—or, as I prefer to call it, a "do tank"—a citizen-empowered organization that will spark greater public awareness and aim to fix some of the problems eroding our living standards.

In the preceding chapters, I outlined a number of specific proposals to reform the major areas of government that impact our quality of life—everything from the way our governments are elected to the systems we use to collect taxes, educate our young and provide health care. In this chapter, I summarize some of those key proposals into one overall plan of action. It is my version of the ideal society, complete with a strategic road map. An ideal society is not just pie-in-the-sky dreaming; to bring it about requires a concrete plan of action, with very specific steps, and a timetable for making it happen.

Naturally, my concept of an ideal society is based on certain values that I consider essential. At the core of those values is my unshakeable belief that the individual is the most vital element of any society. Perhaps I hold this view because I am individualistic by nature. Or perhaps it is because I lived under the totalitarian oppression of the Nazis and the Soviet communists, who made the individual subservient to the state. Either way, I believe that governments, government institutions and social systems all exist primarily to serve the individual, not vice versa. I think we are losing sight of that today more and more.

The following are what I see as the building blocks of a healthy, democratic and economically prosperous society. If we followed this plan of action, there is no doubt in my mind that we could create a broad-based level of wealth and prosperity that would be unlike any other in our history.

STEP 1: FIX THE FLAW IN OUR SYSTEM OF GOVERNMENT

A lot of the problems in society—the build-up of debt, out-of-control spending and bureaucracy, the way government mismanages programs such as health and education and pensions—are all the result of our political system. It has a fundamental flaw, what I call the Achilles' heel of democracy. And the flaw is this: the primary mandate of a politician is to be elected or re-elected, and as a result government decision-making is driven primarily by political considerations rather than by what's best for the country or the economy.

I outlined this problem in Chapter 21, but more important, I propose a solution: the creation of a new chamber of democratically elected Citizen Representatives who would have a significant say in approving major legislation. Citizen Representatives would vote on major bills by way of a secret ballot at the same time as the elected politicians. The two separate sets of votes cast in each chamber would then be added together. A simple majority of votes from both chambers would be required to pass a bill.

Citizen Representatives would hold the balance of power, and their decisions would be based on the long-term social and economic interests of the country, not on political expediency or partisan calculations. By introducing a Chamber of Citizen Representatives, we would finally free ourselves from the destructive grip of political decision-making.

STEP 2: ELIMINATE GOVERNMENT DEBT AND RESTORE BALANCED BUDGETS

Every household, business and farmer knows that they can't spend more money than they bring in or they will eventually go bankrupt. The only group who don't abide by this fundamental law of economics are our politicians. Governments in Western countries have been spending more revenue than they've been taking in for decades now. The result: enormous national debts that threaten to drag down national living standards.

Governments have the power to raise all the money they need through taxation. So why do governments borrow money? And why do banks not only willingly lend governments money but encourage them to borrow even more? The truth of the matter is this arrangement suits both governments and financial institutions. Banks prefer the safety and security of government bonds over riskier investments in private industry, and governments prefer spending borrowed money rather than raising taxes and risking the wrath of the voters.

Governments need to begin balancing their budgets and establishing aggressive debt repayment programs so that future generations aren't burdened with the interest owing on debts racked up by previous governments.

In addition, the citizens of democratic societies in North America and Europe need to handcuff the ability of governments to borrow money by lobbying for legislation that will permanently prevent politicians from spending more revenue than they bring in.

STEP 3: REDUCE GOVERNMENT OVERHEAD

One of the reasons government borrowing and spending is out of control is the unchecked growth of government bureaucracy. The end result is higher taxes on individuals and businesses and a less competitive economic environment. I often use a business analogy to illustrate the problem: if you run a factory, it doesn't matter how productive the workers on the factory floor are if there are too many white collars in the office up top. The business will not be competitive. The same principle holds true for a country.

But no one group of people should be made the scapegoat for the reality that we have become over-governed and over-bureaucratized. It's not the fault of bureaucrats that government has ballooned in size. To a certain extent, we're all to blame: politicians have created endless new government departments, agencies and bureaus, while citizens have sat back and allowed governments to grow unchecked for decades.

In Chapter 18, I spelled out specific proposals for cutting government fat and slashing waste, including targeted cuts that would reduce government spending by 5 to 10 percent per year over a period of five years. By doing so, we could eventually reduce taxes by as much as 50 percent compared with what they are now.

There are no magic bullets or overnight cures. Reducing

government spending requires focus, persistence and an iron-willed determination to straighten out our financial affairs, particularly since there are so many special interests feeding at the government trough. To ensure that the job gets done properly and without any political bias, I would entrust the identification of government waste, duplication and mismanagement to a task force of citizens from a wide range of backgrounds.

STEP 4: REFORM THE TAX SYSTEM

No single aspect of government has a greater impact on productivity and economic growth than the tax system. And yet the tax system in most Western countries is broken: overly complicated and riddled with loopholes, grey areas and privileges for special interests, including the wealthy and the financial institutions that feed off the system.

What's worse, the tax system contains built-in incentives for businesses to close manufacturing operations in their home countries and build products in foreign countries where the social and environmental costs of doing business are far lower. It's one of the main reasons Western countries are moving away from a real economy—one that is based on making tangible products—to a financial economy, which is based predominantly on electronic transactions. However, these financial transactions and manipulations don't create real wealth. In some cases—as we witnessed during the 2008 meltdown—they actually incinerate wealth, wiping out the savings and assets of companies and individuals.

We need a tax system that is totally transparent, simple to administer, easy to understand and with no loopholes—a tax system that could be understood by a high school student and a tax return that is no longer than a single sheet of paper.

In Chapter 18, the solution I put forth is a flat tax. The flat tax rate, which would apply to all personal, corporate and capital income, would start out at around 30 percent but could drop down to as low as 20 percent if we reduced government spending. The flat tax rate would be combined with a consumption tax applied to the purchase of all products and services. With both a flat tax and a consumption tax, there are fewer loopholes and privileges. The rich will end up paying a fairer share of the income tax burden and they would also pay more in consumption taxes, since the total taxes paid on the purchase of a Mercedes would be a lot more than the taxes paid on a Chevy, for example.

If companies choose to invest their profits abroad, they would pay the regular tax rate. But companies that invested profits in their home country by buying new equipment or spending on R & D for new products would not have to pay any taxes whatsoever, since these companies will be stoking the engine of economic growth and job creation.

Tax reform should also recognize that a business is driven by three forces: management, employees and investors, and that all three of these economic stakeholders have a moral right to the financial outcome, or profits, of the business. When employees have a stake in the company's financial success, they are more motivated and more productive. It's been a proven formula at Magna for decades now. That's why I believe businesses that share a minimum 10 percent of their profits with their employees should pay a lower flat tax rate, as an incentive to give a greater number of workers the chance to build capital and even equity in their places of employment. If we fail to turn workers into capitalists, society will inevitably drift toward socialism, with growing cries to take from the rich and give to the poor. Instead, we need to focus on how we can improve the living standards of everyone in society while lifting the people at the very bottom out of poverty and off their dependence on the state.

All of these tax changes are startlingly simple but difficult to push through because of the entrenched interests that live off the present tax system. But once enacted, these tax reforms would do more to fire up the economy than any other single measure.

STEP 5: REFORM THE HEALTH CARE SYSTEM

As a starting point, I believe that in a civilized society every person must have access to basic health care. The health care debate in some Western countries is becoming divided along lines of private care versus public care. But neither of these two systems works: in a completely private system, the poor cannot afford proper care, and in a completely public system, people do not have timely access to medical attention as a result of governments rationing health care dollars and a limited number of health care providers.

I see no reason why a public system and a private system could not co-exist, or why we could not create a hybrid system. To make it work, private health care providers would need to make between 20 to 30 percent of their billings available to the public at government-prescribed public rates. This would relieve the pressure on government funding and would foster greater competition among health care practitioners without removing incentives to earn more. I list some of the ways this could work in Chapter 27.

I also spell out a plan for pushing health care into the workplace as a way to deliver better services at a lower cost—the "better product for a better price" mantra that has propelled my business success. My proposal would bring health care workers directly into the workplace to improve access and services for employees and their families. Another key feature of the workplace proposal would be preventive health care education and learning for employees that would stress the benefits of adopting healthy lifestyle choices. It's a plan that could improve service while at the same time reducing the health care costs paid by employers, individuals and the government—the kind of triple-win scenario I always look for when doing a deal or establishing a new venture.

STEP 6: REFORM THE EDUCATION SYSTEM

I put forth a number of proposals to reform our education system, including a stronger focus on competition and a return to physical fitness and activity, all part of what I refer to as instilling a "sports character" in young people. We also need to place a much heavier emphasis in our schools on nutrition, particularly in the younger grades, and schools should provide at least one nutritious meal each day to students right up until the fourth grade.

In addition, we should stop and ask who's teaching the teachers. A lot of what students learn in school has a strong anti-business bias. Students need to have a greater appreciation for how important business is to society. Without a healthy, functioning economy, we won't have the tax dollars needed to support the many social programs we value, including education itself.

I also argue why we need to promote technical education much more than we currently do. A college or university education is not for everyone, and we also have far too many young people earning degrees that are of little practical value and provide no foundation for a successful career. From the ages 16 to 18, our students should be exposed to a wide range of technical trades, everything from carpentry and electronics to computer repair and automotive mechanics. Exposure to these trades will lead to rewarding careers and good-paying jobs. I believe that many of the best-paying jobs of the future will be those involved in building, designing and repairing products, be it something as big as a house or as small as a lawnmower motor.

And unlike many who believe government should completely subsidize university education, I believe we should cut public funding to the large liberal arts universities and focus government spending instead on smaller, more specialized universities along the lines of what Magna is doing in the automotive industry with the Stronach Centre for Innovation. Some of these specialized universities would focus on learning and research in traditional industries such as manufacturing and agriculture, while others would be geared toward newer industries such as biomedicine and space technology. By creating a number of these smaller, technology-based universities, we could develop and incubate technological innovations as well as advanced materials, processes and production methods. This in turn would help give us a competitive edge in a number of industries, weapons for the global economic warfare that we're engaged in.

In the end, government reforms alone will not solve our social and economic problems. The initiative to find and implement solutions to many of these problems must come from our citizens, from the grassroots of society. And the parameters of a more prosperous society that I've sketched here are not perfect—nothing in the world is, but that shouldn't stop us from striving for perfection and steadily improving what does work along the way. If we enacted the reforms I've outlined above, I believe we could transform our society into one where people take greater responsibility for their lives, where they are more engaged and have more at stake. We would slowly begin to move away from being a society of renters, where people have nothing at stake, to a society of owners. An ownership mentality is a powerful force—it transforms the world around us. You can give the most fruitful and productive land to renters, people with no stake in the ownership or future of the property, and over time the property will likely turn into overgrown bush or desert. But if you give people ownership of some dry and rocky land, they will work to transform it into flourishing gardens full of food and flowers. And so it is with society.

The reforms I've indicated here would generate incredible wealth—enough to improve living standards for a greater number of people than ever before in human history. We have tremendous technologies and advanced knowledge at our fingertips. Yet we are stagnating economically. In some ways, as a society we've become too soft, too complacent. And in other ways, we've lost sight of the principles that made our economies the envy of the world. Going forward, I will dedicate a portion of my time, energy and resources to finding—and implementing—solutions that will restore economic prosperity. And I will encourage others to join me. It's a good cause, one worth fighting for, if only for the sake of our children and our grandchildren.

ACKNOWLEDGEMENTS

Magna would never have become the company it is today were it not for the contributions of a large number of people.

I wish to acknowledge and thank all of the employees who at one time worked for Magna or who continue to work for the company. They are the beating heart of Magna, the people who make it great.

In this book, I tell some of the stories associated with Magna's greatest builders: my good friend and partner Tony Czapka, and his son, Peter, as well as Burt Pabst, Fred Gingl, Herman Koob and Sigi Wolf.

I am grateful for the advice provided over the years by the directors who served on Magna's board, especially Bill Davis, Mike Harris, Jim McCallum, George Hitchman, Don Resnick, Ed Lumley, Royden Richardson, Bill Fike, Franz Vranitzky, Gerhard Randa, Louis Lataif and Lawrence Worrall. Their counsel was invaluable.

I have always enjoyed a strong working relationship with

Magna's executive management, including the current and long-serving executive team of Don Walker, Vince Galifi, Jeff Palmer and Marc Neeb. Don Walker has been an outstanding CEO, and I am confident he will continue to lead Magna forward in the years ahead.

Countless other executives, factory managers and business associates have also contributed greatly to Magna's success over the years, including Brian Colburn, Jim Nicol, Dennis Mills, Jim McAlpine, Tom Skudutis, John Pitrun, Klaus Niemeyer, Heri Polzl, Klaus Bytzek, Max Amtmann, Cam Smith, Frank Vasilkioti and Alon Ossip.

I wish to thank Magna's many customers—in particular, the representatives of the world's major automotive manufacturers who gave Magna the opportunity to bid on new contracts and who rewarded us over the years with their business. We were always motivated by the desire to give them a better product for a better price.

I would also like to thank Paul Pivato, who has worked with me for the past twenty-five years. Paul took the many experiences I've had, as well as my business philosophies and proposals for socio-economic reform, and helped me fine-tune them in writing *The Magna Man*.

G   P   S/S